CHURCH LIFE AND THOUGHT
IN NORTH AFRICA
A.D. 200

The Tombstone of S. Perpetua, S. Felicitas, and their comrades.

CHURCH LIFE AND THOUGHT
IN NORTH AFRICA
A.D. 200

by

STUART A. DONALDSON, D.D.

Master of Magdalene College, Cambridge

Cambridge :
at the University Press
1909

CAMBRIDGE UNIVERSITY PRESS
Cambridge, New York, Melbourne, Madrid, Cape Town,
Singapore, São Paulo, Delhi, Mexico City

Cambridge University Press
The Edinburgh Building, Cambridge CB2 8RU, UK

Published in the United States of America by Cambridge University Press, New York

www.cambridge.org
Information on this title: www.cambridge.org/9781107652767

First published 1909
First paperback edition 2013

A catalogue record for this publication is available from the British Library

ISBN 978-1-107-65276-7 Paperback

MATRI
ET
UXORI

PREFACE

MY aim in writing the following pages has been twofold. On the one hand I have had in view those whom Tertullian calls "Simple folk—not to say ignorant and unlettered—who ever form the majority of Believing Christians[1]"; and I have endeavoured for their sake to draw a picture of the Church Life and Thought of North Africa in Tertullian's time, which will not demand a knowledge of Latin or Greek, nor call for more than the most elementary acquaintance with the problems of Church History: for their sake, I have made it a rule to translate all my references from Greek or Latin into English. On the other hand, I have not been without hopes that the passages I have tabulated in support of my statements may serve as a *catena* of references for the more serious student of Theology: I have therefore also made it a rule to subjoin in each case the original words of the passage translated.

---

[1] Simplices quique—ne dixerim imprudentes et idiotae—quae major semper credentium pars est. *adv. Prax.* III.

In this way, I trust that this Essay may serve the double purpose of assisting those who are entering upon a serious study of Early Church History, and also of interesting a wider public. The search into the developments of Christian Doctrine and Practice in the Church of North Africa, as shewn particularly in the writings of Tertullian, has proved a delightful subject for myself: I hope it may be so to others also.

STUART A. DONALDSON.

THE LODGE,
   MAGDALENE COLLEGE,
    CAMBRIDGE.

     November 20th, 1909.

I wish to express my thanks to the Divinity Professors, and especially to the Regius Professor of Divinity, in the University of Cambridge, for much kindness and many valuable suggestions. The Essay was submitted to them as a *Thesis* for the D.D. degree.

I should like also to say how much I owe to the unfailing courtesy and patience of the authorities of the University Press.

I have to acknowledge my obligations to the following books, viz. :

Oehler's edition of *The Works of Tertullian*. (3 volumes, Weigel, Leipzig. 1854.)

Bishop Kaye's *Account of the Writings of Tertullian*. (Rivingtons. 3rd edn. 1845.)

Prof. Bigg's *The Church's Task under the Roman Empire*. (Clarendon Press. 1905.)

—— *The Origins of Christianity*. Ed. T. B. Strong. (Clarendon Press. 1909.)

Glover's *Conflict of Religions in the Early Roman Empire*. (Methuen. 1909.)

Bindley's edition of Tertullian's *Apology*. (Clarendon Press. 1889.)

—— Translation with introduction &c. of Tertullian's *Apology*. (Parker. 1890.)

Woodham's edition of Tertullian's *Apology*. (Deighton. 1850.)

Monceaux's *Tertullien et les Origines*. (First Volume of *Histoire Littéraire de l'Afrique Chrétienne*.) (Leroux, Paris. 1901.)

Leclercq's *L'Afrique Chrétienne*. (Lecoffre, Paris. 1904.)

Adhémar d'Alès' *La Théologie de Tertullien*. (Beauchesne, Paris. 1905.)

Guignebert's *Tertullien : Étude sur ses sentiments à l'égard de l'Empire et de la Société civile*. (Leroux, Paris. 1901.)

Kolberg's *Verfassung, Cultus, und Disciplin der christlichen Kirche nach den Schriften Tertullians*. (Wichert, Braunsberg. 1886.)

Smith's *Dictionary of Christian Biography*, s.v. Tertullianus, Montanus etc.

Cabrol's *Dictionnaire d'Archéologie Chrétienne*, s.v. Africa.

Cumont's *Mysteries of Mithra*, English Translation. (Kegan Paul, Trench, Trübner and Co., London. 1903.)

Bethune Baker's *Introduction to Early History of Christian Doctrine*. (Methuen. 1903.)

Dill's *Roman Society from Nero to M. Aurelius*. (Macmillan, London. 1904.)

Various magazine articles, and especially some by Professor Swete in the *Journ. Theol. Studies* and elsewhere.

TABLE OF CONTENTS

CHAPTER			PAGE
I.	INTRODUCTORY.		1
II.	SOURCES OF INFORMATION.		10
III.	TERTULLIAN.		21
IV.	THE CHURCH IN NORTH AFRICA IN TERTULLIAN'S TIME.		
	§ i.	Church Government. The Threefold order of ministry. The position of the Laity.	42
	§ ii.	Baptism.	54
	§ iii.	The *Agape*.	66
	§ iv.	The Eucharist.	70
	§ v.	Prayer.	
		a. The *de Oratione*.	80
		b. Turning to the East in Prayer. .	83
		c. Attitude in Prayer. . . .	83
		d. Prayers for the dead. . . .	86
	§ vi.	Penance and the Forgiveness of Sins. .	88
	§ vii.	Liturgy.	92
	§ viii.	The Creed.	96
	§ ix.	The Cross.	101
	§ x.	The Jews in North Africa. . . .	105
	§ xi.	Heresy and Heretics.	110
	§ xii.	The Doctrine of the Holy Trinity. .	119

CHAPTER							PAGE
V.	NORTH AFRICAN MARTYRS.						
	§ i.	The Scillitan Martyrs. .	.	.	.		124
	§ ii.	The Passion of S. Perpetua. .		.	.		128
VI.	THE RIVALS OF CHRISTIANITY.		.	.	.		138
	§ i.	The Cult of Isis. .	.	.	.	.	139
	§ ii.	The Cult of Mithra.	.	.	.	.	148
	§ iii.	Caesar Worship. .	.	.	.	.	158
VII.	MONTANISM.	.	.	.	.	.	166
VIII.	THE "OCTAVIUS" OF MINUCIUS FELIX. .				.		173
IX.	THE BIBLE IN NORTH AFRICA.	.	.	.		179
X.	RECAPITULATORY.	.	.	.	.	.	183
	APPENDIX. LIST OF TERTULLIAN'S WORKS						
	WITH PROBABLE DATES.	.	.	.	.		192
	INDEX I. General .	.	.	.	.	.	195
	II. List of quotations from the writings						
	of Tertullian	.	.	.	.		198

PHOTOGRAPHS.

Tombstone of Perpetua.	.	.	.	.	*Frontispiece*
View of Timgad .	.	.	.	.	between pp. 2 and 3
The Theatre, Carthage	.	.	.	.	to face p. 33
The Amphitheatre	.	.	.	.	.	to face p. 124
"Salvum lotum !"	.	.	.	.	.	to face p. 133

CHAPTER I

INTRODUCTORY

UNDER the term "North Africa" we must include not only the Roman Province of Africa, but also the Kingdoms of Numidia and Mauretania, all of which came more or less under the influence of Roman Rule and shared in the advantages as well as the disadvantages incident thereto. The Dictator, C. Julius Caesar, had done much to reorganize the government of the country; in fact as Mommsen truly says, "Latin Africa is not much less his work than Latin Gaul." On the destruction of Carthage in B.C. 146, the Roman Province of Africa had been constituted : to this Caesar added part of Numidia, and "the old and the new Africa" included not only the modern state of Tunis, but also Tripoli and the French Province of Constantine : and this remained the constitution of the Roman Province until the end of the reign of Tiberius. In the year 37 A.D. it was arranged that the coast-land from Hippo (*Bona*) eastward to Cyrene should be called Africa and placed under the direction of the Proconsul : whereas the western part of the Province including Cirta (*Constantine*) the capital, and all the great military camps in the interior, was to be placed under the commander of the African Legion.

The immediate result of this was the rapid development of the country. Under the skilful care of the Roman government, large permanent camps for the maintenance of their troops were prepared, connected with one another by roads, and before the end of the first century A.D. North Africa became one of the most populous, fertile, and highly cultivated regions of the Roman Empire. Carthage itself was indisputably the second city of the Latin half of the Empire: next to Rome it was the most lively, perhaps also the most corrupt, city of the West, and the most important centre of Latin culture and literature.

From Carthage radiated the network of roads, traces of which still survive after more than 1000 years of Mussulman rule: and travellers to-day in Tunis and Algeria are amazed at the evidences of Roman civilization and power which meet them at every turn. Theveste (*Tebessa*) 190 miles S.W. of Carthage was a military centre of great importance: founded during the reign of Vespasian it was the headquarters of the Third Augustan Legion and the centre of defence against the inroads of Berbers, standing as it did at the junction of nine roads. Towards the end of the second century A.D. it was surpassed in its wealth and importance only by Carthage, and under Septimius

Timgad (Thamugas).

Severus it reached a high degree of prosperity and became the central trade depôt of the country. About 100 miles due west of Theveste, we reach the "Pompeii" of Africa, Timgad, ancient *Thamugadis* or *Thamugas*, a colony apparently founded by Trajan, and handed over to the Thirtieth Legion, the Ulpia Victrix, to recompense its veterans for their share in his victory over the Parthians, and also as entrusting them with a position of great military importance. (A general view of the present condition of the remains is given in the adjoining photograph.) Eighteen or nineteen miles west of Timgad, on the way to Batna, lies another important military centre, Lambèse (*Lambessa*, or *Lambaesis*), built about 169 A.D. as the new headquarters of the Third Augustan Legion, ultimately becoming a city of some 60,000 inhabitants, and the headquarters of the Roman army. It was in immediate communication with Cirta, Calama (*Gelma*), and Hippo Regius (*Bona*), as well as with stations to the south towards the desert; the modern El Kantara (*Calceus Herculis*), and Biskra (*Beskera*), and eastwards to Ain Khenschla (*Mascula*), one of Trajan's colonies. In fact the whole country bears on every side marked traces of Roman vigour and enterprise, even after the long period of Arab domination, and the great importance of the district to the Roman Empire is very clearly brought to the notice of everyone who travels there to-day.

The N. and N.W. portions of the province of Africa were the great corn-producing areas: even in the time of Augustus, while one third of Roman corn came from Egypt, another third was sent by North Africa. Later on, in the fourth century, Africa was the chief source of the oil used for Roman baths, though it was of inferior quality to that from Italy and Spain, less skill being used in its preparation. We also find that the export trade of horses and cattle from Numidia and Mauretania was extensive. Altogether, it is difficult to overestimate the importance of the part played by N. Africa of the second and third centuries in the development of European history: for although geo-graphically part of Africa, Tunis and Algeria really belong to Europe: a fact which is delightfully brought home to the reader in Mr Belloc's brilliant Essay, *Esto Perpetua*.

Thus North Africa must be understood to be that part of Africa which the Arabs, with their eye for the configuration of natural features, have called Djezirat-el-Maghreb, "The Isle of the West," a district with the modern Tunis for its centre, jutting out from the African continent towards Sicily and Italy, bounded on the north by the Mediterranean, on the south and east by the desert of the Sahara, and on the west by the Atlantic ocean. The great range of Atlas runs along its whole course from east to west, causing the country to look northwards towards Europe, rather

than southwards towards Africa: it is in fact an
" annexe of Europe," and since the foundation by the
Phoenicians of its metropolis Carthage, with its com-
manding position on what is now the Bay of Tunis, its
history has had to do with Europe and the basin of the
Mediterranean rather than with its own continent.

After nearly 150 years of rivalry and conflict,
Carthage had been obliged to submit to the might
of Rome, but before long she had reappeared after
her eclipse, and resumed her position as one of the
world-centres of trade, though she could be no longer
formidable as a military power.

It was doubtless through Carthage that Christianity
reached the interior, and found there almost as
wonderful a fusion of races as go to make up the
Anglo-Saxons. Not to speak of the aboriginal Libyans,
who appear so little in history that they may be passed
by, we find the " African " type consists of an inter-
fusion of indigenous Berbers and Moors on the one
hand, with Phoenicians and Europeans—Italians or
Greeks—on the other: these again naturally divided
themselves into men of the mountain, the plain, and
the sea coast, each with their marked characteristics,
and each contributing their share to the development
of the national type.

So far as the Church of North Africa is concerned,
we find its whole genius summarized as well as typified
in the three great names of Tertullian, Cyprian and

Augustine : apart from these three, though it produced men of action, it gave to the world no great thinker, no great poet, no great representative of literature[1]. But these three leaders are enough in themselves to redeem any society from the charge of being ordinary or commonplace, and are indicative of the strong vitality that underlay the quiet surface of the national life.

Mommsen has well said (*Prov. Rom. Emp.* vol. II. p. 343) "In the development of Christianity Africa plays the very first part: if it arose in Syria, it was in and through Africa that it became the religion for the world...If Christianity was by the destruction of the Jewish Church-state released from its Jewish basis, it became the religion of the world by the fact, that in the great world-empire it began to speak the universally current imperial language : and those nameless men, who since the second century Latinized the Christian writings...were in part Italians, but above all Africans. In Africa, to all appearance, the knowledge of Greek, which is able to dispense with translations, was far more seldom to be met with than at least in Rome : and, on the other hand, the oriental element, that preponderated particularly in the early stages of Christianity, here found a readier reception than in the other Latin-speaking lands of the west.

---

[1] The writer is not forgetful of the claims of Arnobius, Lactantius, and Apuleius.

Even as regards the polemic literature called especially
into existence by the new faith, since the Roman
Church at this epoch belonged to the Greek circle,
Africa took the lead in the Latin tongue. The whole
Christian authorship down to the end of this period is,
so far as it is Latin, African: Tertullian and Cyprian
were from Carthage, Arnobius from Sicca, Lactantius,
and probably in like manner Minucius Felix, were, in
spite of their classic Latin, Africans, and not less the
somewhat later Augustine. In Africa the growing
Church found its most zealous confessors, and its most
gifted defenders. For the literary conflict of the Faith
Africa furnished by far the most and the ablest com-
batants, whose special characteristics, now in eloquent
discussion, now in witty ridicule of fables, now in
vehement indignation, found a true and mighty field
for their display in the onslaught on the old gods."

Ethnographically, the aboriginals of "North Africa"
are to be distinguished most sharply from the Blacks of
the south and also from the Egyptians of the east.
They appear near Tangier as Amâzigh, in the Sahara
as Imôshagh, as Maxyes at the foundation of Carthage,
as Mazices in the Roman period: but however marked
may have been their characteristics in early days, they
are hardly to be distinguished now from the many and
various stocks with which they have intermingled.
The origin of the generic term Afer and the name
Africa is unknown; all we can say is that it is the name

applied to all the inhabitants of the continent lying over against Sicily, especially to the Phoenicians. Libyans is the term applied to the easterly tribes, coming in contact with Egypt. Numidians (= *Nomades*) is the name associated most with King Masinissa: the name Mauri is restricted to the inhabitants of the western portion of the sea-board, the Gaetulians lying to the S. of the Mauri. Berber is the generic term applied originally on their arrival by the Arabs to the northern tribes, and now including all of non-Arabic descent, among whom may be especially mentioned the Kabyles. The Berber language has survived even to the present day: on the other hand, the Phoenicians, who from Carthage dominated N. Africa for some 600 years, have left no public document extant after the time of Tiberius, though their language was in use till the end of the fourth century. It is Latin which takes the place of Punic as the official tongue, and not Greek, as already noticed. This we find to be the case too with Punic urban organization: though it was at first adopted by the Romans for their government of the country, it gradually gave way to " Italian Rights," as we see in the case of Utica, under Julius Caesar and Augustus: and this form of government was much extended under Trajan.

The bulk of the population to-day is Arab: these, as their name implies, came from Arabia, and overran the country in the middle of the seventh century A.D.

Since then Christianity has only been allowed to exist on sufferance, and the high degree of civilization and prosperity attained under the Roman Rule was lost, never to be regained till now. To-day, under the care of France, there is good prospect of N. Africa resuming her old position of importance : the varied beauty and attractiveness of her country, the healthiness of her climate, and the resources of her soil, lead one to hope that this prospect may be realized, and that this delightful region may once more take its part in the History of Europe, to which rather than to the "Dark Continent" it rightly belongs.

CHAPTER II

SOURCES OF INFORMATION

THE Church in North Africa at the end of the second
and beginning of the third century presents itself to
us in the writings of Tertullian as an organization complete and matured, full of life and vigour, progressive
and hopeful. But we are baffled when we try to outline
the birth and gradual development of this vigorous
community. It is possible that Christianity was introduced into Carthage from the East, with which it had
numerous ties through trade and commerce; while it
had special relations with the metropolis of the
Empire, it cannot be said that it owed its Christianity
to Rome more than to Antioch or Alexandria or Jerusalem itself[1].

[1] At the same time it must be remembered that Tertullian asserts
that African Christianity owed much to Rome. He says, while
urging Heretics to bow to the authority of Apostolic churches, "If
you are near Italy, you have Rome, where there is for us also an
authority close at hand....See what it has learnt, what it has
taught, and what it has held also in common with the churches of
Africa." He then proceeds to summarize the chief points of Faith
and practice common to both. (Si autem Italiae adjaces, habes
Romam, unde nobis quoque auctoritas praesto est....Videamus quid
didicerit, quid docuerit, cum Africanis quoque ecclesiis contesserarit.
de Praes. Haeret. xxxvi.)

The evidence of French excavations at Tunis shews that for some time Jews and Christians used common cemeteries, and so must have lived more or less amicably together: but this state of affairs did not last long, and by Tertullian's time we find the Jews among the most vehement persecutors of the Christians. "All outside the Christian Faith are its enemies, especially the Jews," he says, "in consequence of their jealous rivalry[1]."

To the outside Gentile world, there was often confusion between Jews and Christians, and either sect often found it necessary to disclaim connexion with the other: but there seems no reason to doubt that in Carthage, as in other parts of the world, the regular annual visits of Jews to Jerusalem kept up a close connexion between those two centres, and at an early date introduced at least a knowledge of Christian Faith and practice into the Province of Africa.

Whatever its origin, there can be no doubt that once introduced Christianity made rapid progress in North Africa, and this is perhaps largely due to the fact that underlying all their polytheism, the Pagans of that district had firmly grasped the idea of a supreme Deity, and so were ready to welcome the monotheism of Christianity, with its high ethical standard of teaching and conduct.

For an investigation into the condition of the

[1] Tot hostes ejus (sc. disciplinae) quot extranei, et quidem proprie ex aemulatione Judaei. *Apol.* vii.

Christian Church in North Africa, we have three chief
sources of information: (1) Inscriptions: (2) Buildings:
(3) Writings. As our present enquiry concerns only
the condition of the Church about the year 200 A.D.
these sources of information become much curtailed:
(3) practically resolves itself into the writings of Tertullian, (2) is non-existent, except in the cemeteries,
(1) can give us but few examples, and they are often
of doubtful value.

(1) *Inscriptions.* There are two epitaphs which
seem to be undoubtedly Christian and to belong to our
period. First, there is the inscription of Rasinia
Secunda who died at Tipasa A.D. 238 (*C.I.L.* VIII. 9289)[1]

> RASINIA
>
> SECVNDA
>
> REDD. XVI
>
> KAL. NOVEM.
>
> P. CLXXXXVIIII

(Rasinia Secunda redd(-idit spiritum) XVI Kalend.
Novembres, (anno) P(rovinciae) 199=238 A.D.).

Secondly, there is the epitaph of a Christian
Lady as her name shews, who was buried at Giufi
(= *Henscher Mscherga*) before the year 227 A.D. Her
husband was perhaps connected with the Proconsul
C. Quintilius Marcellus. The inscription runs thus:

---

[1] See Leclercq, *L'Afrique Chrétienne,* I. p. 51.

PESCENNIA QVOD VVL (*sic*) DEVS

H. M. F. BONIS NATALIBVS

NATA . MATRONALITER

NVPTA . VXOR CASTA

MATER PIA GENVIT FILI

OS . III . ET FILIAS . II . VIXIT

ANNIS . XXX . $\bar{\text{P}}$. VICTORI

NA . VIXIT . ANNIS . VII . $\bar{\text{P}}$.

SVNNIVS . VIXIT . ANNIS

III . $\bar{\text{P}}$. MARCVS VIXIT

ANNIS . II . $\bar{\text{P}}$. MARCEL

LVS . VIXIT . ANNV . I . $\bar{\text{P}}$. FO

RTVNATA . VIXIT . ANNIS

XIII . M . VIII . $\bar{\text{P}}$ MARCEL

LVS CONIVGI DIGNAE

SED ET FILIS FILIABVS

QVE NOSTRIS ME VI

VO MEMORIAM FECI

OMNIBVS ESSE PERENNEM[1].

" Pescennia God's-will—*honestae memoriae femina*—a lady of honourable memory—well born—duly wedded —a chaste wife—an affectionate mother—bore three sons and two daughters and died aged 30 : her children were Pescennia Victorina who lived seven years : Pescennius Sunnius lived three years : P. Marcus two : P. Marcellus one : P. Fortunata 13 years and eight months. I, Pescennius Marcellus who survive them, have erected this

[1] *C.I.L.* viii. 870.

tombstone to be an everlasting memorial for all to see, to my dearest wife and our sons and daughters[1]." It is worth noticing that a similar phrase was used a few years previously to describe the Martyr S. Perpetua: *Vibia Perpetua, honeste nata, liberaliter instituta, matronaliter nupta*[2].

Such inscriptions as the foregoing do not take us very far into the inner life of the North African Christians of our period, though the second reveals the fact that a Roman of high rank could have a Christian wife and be tenderly devoted to her: whether he also himself was Christian, does not appear[3].

(2) *Buildings.* There were no buildings used exclusively as churches in North Africa at the beginning of the third century, but cemeteries, like the catacombs at Rome, formed the first meeting places

[1] Leclercq, *l.c.* p. 52.

[2] See the Dean of Westminster's *Passion of S. Perpetua*, p. 62.

[3] Tertullian mentions another Proconsul, Claudius Lucius Herminianus (or Gerominianus) of Cappadocia, who had a Christian wife, and in consequence persecuted the Christians. Suffering from some loathsome disease which bred worms, and deserted by all in his palace, he exclaimed, "Let no one know of this, lest Christian men rejoice and Christian women hope." Afterwards, he acknowledged that he had been wrong in forcing Believers under torture to abjure their faith, and died "almost a Christian." (Claudius Lucius Herminianus in Cappadocia, cum, indigne ferens uxorem suam ad hanc sectam transisse, Christianos crudeliter tractasset, solusque in praetorio suo vastatus peste convivis vermibus ebullisset, "nemo sciat," aiebat, "ne gaudeant Christiani aut sperent Christianae." Postea, cognito errore suo, quod tormentis quosdam a proposito suo excidere fecisset, paene Christianus decessit. *ad Scap.* III.)

of the Christians, both for retirement and for worship. The excavations of French archaeologists have revealed many interesting points, and we owe much to the enthusiasm and zeal of the White Fathers, a missionary order instituted by Cardinal Lavigerie, to whom and especially to Père Delattre is due the establishment of the museum at Carthage, with its unique collection of discoveries made in the neighbourhood: these throw light not only upon Punic, Greek, and Roman history, but also give us priceless information as to the customs and life of Christians in North Africa during a prolonged period[1].

As has been pointed out by many writers—notably Sir William Ramsay—the early Christians earned their recognition as a legally constituted body in the eyes of the state by enrolling themselves as members of a Burial Club: their cemeteries were recognized as the lawful property of the community, and they themselves

---

[1] In his brochure *Un Pèlerinage aux ruines de Carthage et au musée Lavigerie* (J. Poncet, 18 Rue François-Dauphin, Lyon) Père Delattre quotes several Christian inscriptions found in various places, but particularly in the Great Basilica of Damous-el-Karita. Here have been discovered more than 14,000 fragments of Christian epitaphs, containing more than 400 different names (p. 106), but as these necessarily belong to a period later than A.D. 200, they must not detain us here. Among those specially named however by Père Delattre (p. 63) we notice

QVOD VVLT DEVS
FIDELIS IN PACE

a parallel to the epitaph of Pescennia quoted above.

were allowed to assemble at the spot where their dead lay buried; and so for North Africa at least the cemeteries—*areae*—became the first churches, and the tombs of martyrs the first altars: though it must be remembered that there was neither church nor altar proper, till a much later date. We find therefore that the first cry of the populace in time of persecution was "away with the cemeteries!" and Tertullian with bitter play upon the word, which means "threshing floor" as well as "cemetery," says "No state can tolerate with impunity the shedding of Christian blood: in the procuratorship of Hilarianus[1] when the people shouted, with reference to the fields belonging to our burial places, 'Away with the burial fields' (*areae*), their own fields (*areae*) suffered: for they gathered in none of their crops[2]."

A good example of one of these *areae* has been excavated at a place called Cherchel some 60 or 70 miles west of Algiers on the coast (the ancient *Caesarea* near Tenez—ancient *Cartennae*) which apparently belongs to our period, the time of the persecutions of Septimius Severus. Here we find the burial ground (*hortus*) in the middle of which is a small enclosure of some 30 yards by 15, surrounded by a lofty wall, and

---

[1] Under whom SS. Perpetua and Felicitas suffered, A.D. 203.

[2] *ad Scap.* III. Doleamus necesse est, quod nulla civitas impune latura sit sanguinis nostri effusionem: sicut et sub Hilariano praeside, cum de areis sepulturarum nostrarum adclamassent, Areae non sint! areae ipsorum non fuerunt: messes enim suas non egerunt.

only accessible by a single door (*area muro cincta*, or *area martyrum*, or *casa major*). This formed a veritable sanctuary, in the centre of which is found a vaulted shrine (*cella*) covering the tombstone of a martyr which takes the shape of a table (*mensa*). At this table as at an altar was celebrated the Eucharist, the officiating clergy taking up their position under the vaulted dome, as in a kind of apse, the congregation standing all round outside[1]. Such seems to have been the earliest form of church in North Africa, whither the Christian community could betake themselves outside the city walls, and find privacy, and in case of need a safe refuge.

But besides these *areae* there must also have been a common meeting place within the city itself, probably the actual house where the bishop lived, or some hall in connexion with it. It must be this to which Tertullian refers when (in *de Virgin. vel.* XIII.) he argues that unmarried girls who wear the veil of their virginity *in the streets*, ought also to wear it *in church*, where it seems to have been the custom, at Carthage at least, for virgins to attend unveiled: " As they veil their head among the heathen, in church they certainly should hide their maidenhood which they conceal outside of the church. They are afraid of outsiders, they say: let them reverence also the brethren: or else let them be consistent and dare to be seen as virgins in the streets also, as they do in church....Why do they hide away

[1] Monceaux, I. p. 14: Leclercq, I. p. 58.

their advantages abroad, but make them public in church[1]?" That this custom was not universal, but varied in different churches, appears from a passage in *de Orat.* XXI. "But this point must be dealt with, which is observed differently in different churches as a matter of uncertainty: I mean, whether virgins ought to be veiled or not (*sc.* in church)[2]."

Tertullian speaks of the church as an actual edifice in *de Pudic.* IV. where he says that the excommunication of gross and unnatural offenders against morality is "not only from the threshold of the church but from the whole building[3]."

Although the Christians of North Africa erected no buildings specially set apart as churches for another century, yet even in Tertullian's time, in the *atria* of the private houses where meetings were held, it would seem that special seats of honour were reserved for the clergy[4]: we read in *de Exhort. Castit.* VII. "The

[1] Ut apud ethnicos caput velant, certe in ecclesia virginitatem suam abscondant quam extra ecclesiam celant. Timent extraneos, revereantur et fratres : aut constanter audeant et in vicis virgines videri, sicut audent in ecclesiis....Quo ergo foris quidem bonum suum abstrudunt, in ecclesia vero provulgant?

[2] Sed quod promiscue observatur per ecclesias quasi incertum, id retractandum est, velarine debeant virgines an non. The whole discussion of course turns on the interpretation of 1 Cor. xi. 2—16.

[3] Reliquas autem libidinum furias impias et in corpora et in sexus ultra jura naturae, non modo limine verum omni ecclesiae tecto submovemus, quia non sunt delicta sed monstra.

[4] Monceaux, p. 16.

authority of the church has arranged a difference between the clergy and the laity and a sanctified dignity is added by the special seats allotted to the clergy[1]."

He seems to imply the existence of an altar in several passages, *e.g. de orat.* XXVIII. " We are the true worshippers and the true priests, who praying in the spirit, in the spirit offer up prayer as a sacrifice, a victim peculiarly acceptable unto God....This victim we ought to bring with whole hearted devotion, fed by faith, nurtured on truth, of spotless innocence, and blameless chastity, crowned with the Agape, accompanied by a train of good works amid psalms and hymns to the altar of God, sure to obtain from God all our requests[2]." So *ibid.* XIX. " Will not your fast day be all the more solemn, if you also stand at God's altar[3] ? " In another passage *ibid.* XI. we have allusion to S. Matt. v. 23 f. " We must not go up to the altar of God, until we have reconciled any discord or cause of offence between ourselves and our brethren[4]."

[1] Differentiam inter ordinem et plebem constituit ecclesiae auctoritas, et honor per ordinis consessum sanctificatus.

[2] Nos sumus veri adoratores et veri sacerdotes, qui spiritu orantes spiritu sacrificamus orationem hostiam Dei propriam et acceptabilem...Hanc de toto corde devotam, fide pastam, veritate curatam, innocentia integram, castitate mundam, agape coronatam cum pompa operum bonorum inter psalmos et hymnos deducere ad Dei altare debemus, omnia nobis a Deo impetraturam.

[3] Nonne solemnior erit statio tua, si et ad aram Dei steteris?

[4] Ne prius ascendamus ad altare Dei, quam si quid discordiae vel offensae cum fratribus contraxerimus resolvamus.

(3) *Writings.* Tertullian is here the chief source of our information, and a more detailed account of him and his writings must be reserved till the next chapter. A full list of his extant works will be found in the Appendix.

CHAPTER III

TERTULLIAN

No one has ever ventured to class Tertullian among the "Saints": in some respects his life was anything but saintly, and he ended it by becoming the vigorous opponent of the orthodox Church for which he had done so much. He would be the last to claim the title for himself: he is very conscious of his own shortcomings which he laments on several occasions. Nevertheless in my opinion he deserves to be called a Saint for his whole-hearted devotion to highest ideals, his uncompromising demand for truth in all his enquiries, and his passionate love for the person of Christ; at all events, no one would refuse him his place as a Leader of thought and religious life.

There can be no doubt that the Church at large and particularly the Western Church owes him a debt of gratitude which is quite inestimable: for to him, more than to most, is due the orderly logical position of Christian thought, and even the very language whereby the statement of that position is rendered possible. I hope to make this claim good by what follows, and also to shew what an impetus the preaching of the Gospel and the spread of Christianity received at the end of the second century of our era from the vigorous personality, the burning zeal, and the remarkable abilities of this gifted man.

Of the actual facts of his life, there is not much to say. His full name was Q. Septimius Florens Tertullianus, and he seems to have been the son of a "proconsular centurion" resident at Carthage[1]. We may assign the date of his birth to about the year 160 A.D. and the city of his birth, Carthage, probably provided him with his early education. It was at Carthage that he spent most of his days, and it was there that he found the scene of his manifold activities. There can be no doubt that he passed part of his youth at Rome, where he must have studied law to some purpose: for though there is no evidence that he practised as a jurisconsult, his knowledge of Roman law is minute and intimate, as appears again and again from his writings.

In all probability he was born a pagan, but he must have been converted to Christianity before 195 A.D. Not long after his conversion he published his famous *Apologeticum*, perhaps in the year 197, of which more presently. There is some reason to think that he

---

[1] So S. Jerome, *de vir. illus.* 53. Bp Kaye explains the term "Proconsular Centurion" as an "officer who was constantly in attendance of the Proconsul to receive his commands" (p. 6, n.).

was ordained priest in or about the year 200, and that by the year 213 he had joined the Montanists and was ranked as a heretic by the orthodox. After that, dates become very uncertain: Jerome speaks of his dying in extreme old age but we are unable to place his death more definitely than by saying that it occurred between 220 and 240.

He was a prolific writer and his authentic works still extant number no fewer than 31[1], some of which are of considerable length: but throughout these writings, historical allusions are singularly few, and we possess but scanty *data* for reconstructing the events of his life. Of that life however it is clear that the key-note was his constant struggle against what he felt to be wrong: he was a fighter by nature and by training, and he went straight at his point without fear of consequences or thought of style: his abilities, learning, and memory were prodigious: his versatility immense. But he lacked sense of proportion, and had no critical judgment to keep him straight in the midst of his polemics.

With these few preliminary remarks, we may turn to the examination of his writings and attempt to reconstruct the man from what he says himself. But before doing so it will be well to say a word or two about the historical setting of his life.

The Roman empire was already shewing symptoms

[1] See Appendix.

of that decay which was ere long to culminate in due disaster. The emperors of the second century, able administrators, capable generals, to a large extent honest and true-hearted patriots, such as Trajan, Hadrian, Antoninus Pius, and Marcus Aurelius, had been succeeded in 180 by the son of the last named, Commodus, the worthless offspring of a worthy sire : on the last day of the year 192 poison had been administered to him by his mistress Marcia, but as it failed to act he had been strangled by a professional wrestler. After that follows a period of stress and turmoil from which the African soldier known to us as Septimius Severus eventually emerges and makes good his title to be emperor. His rivals Pertinax, Didius Julianus, Niger, and Albinus one after another disappear, the first two murdered, the two others defeated in battle. Septimius Severus, who was born in Leptis in North Africa, is an emperor of special interest to us, as he spent the last four years of his life in Britain and died at York Feb. 4, 211. He left the empire to his sons Caracalla and Geta, and in the following year the elder, Caracalla, murdered his brother Geta in the arms of his mother Julia Domna, who was herself wounded by her own son in attempting to save his brother. Caracalla was himself assassinated in 217.

Commodus had given his subjects so much to occupy their attention by his extravagances and eccentricities that they had not paid much attention to the

Christians while he lived. But Severus' edict of 202[1] forbidding both Jews and Christians to proselytize gave those who hated Christianity in the provinces an excuse for interference, and persecution became a conspicuous feature in the daily experience of Christians in North Africa.

Traces of these turbulent times are very evident throughout Tertullian's writings, and his strenuous life and character fit in well with his surroundings. Carthage the scene of his birth and life-work was of course one of the most important towns on the southern seaboard of the Mediterranean, and in the earlier days had been a formidable rival of Rome herself as mistress of the world. Even to-day its modern representative Tunis under French protection and guidance is a place of considerable importance, and may be increasingly so as time goes on, strategically, commercially, and imperially. In Tertullian's day it was the seat of the Roman government of North Africa, and by the strength of its position, the variety of its trade interests, and the attractiveness of its sunny climate, drew to itself a vast population, not only Phoenician—Carthage according to tradition was founded from Tyre and Sidon—not only indigenous Berbers,

---

[1] Recorded by Spartian, who wrote under Diocletian nearly 100 years later. *Vita Severi*, XVII. In itinere Palaestinis plurima jura fundavit. Judaeos fieri sub gravi poena vetuit: idem etiam de Christianis sanxit.

Numidians and Moors from Africa itself, but also inhabitants of all parts of the Mediterranean, a veritable congeries of manifold languages and nationalities.

By the time of Tertullian Christianity had become a very important factor in the life of the Province of North Africa. Cyprian, Bishop of Carthage, writing in 256 (*Ep.* LXXIII.) speaks of the presence of no fewer than 71 bishops from proconsular Africa and Numidia gathered at the first council of Carthage about 220 A.D. and in the same letter he mentions that 84 bishops had been present at a synod held the previous year, A.D. 255. Tertullian's own words on the subject may be rhetorical, but there must be a substratum of truth : he says " (The Romans) loudly declare that their state is beset, that Christians meet them everywhere, in the country, in the walled villages, in the islands : they lament, as though it were to their own loss, that both sexes, all ages and conditions of men, even all ranks, are crossing over to this name[1]." Again, " We are but of yesterday, and we have filled all that belongs to you, your cities, your islands, your villages, your borough towns, your councils, even your camps, your tribes, decuries, palace, senate, forum. We

---

[1] Obsessam vociferantur civitatem ; in agris, in castellis, in insulis Christianos : omnem sexum, aetatem, condicionem etiam dignitatem transgredi ad hoc nomen quasi detrimento moerent. *Apol.* I.

have only left you your temples. We can count your
armies: (the Christians) of a single province will be
found to be more numerous[1]." Again, he speaks of the
Christians as "So vast a multitude, almost the majority
in each state[2]," and once more, he says, "There is no
race to-day which is not Christian[3]." The Gospel had
even penetrated the wilds of Britain, "inaccessible
to the Romans, but subdued by Christ[4]." And there
are several other passages to the same effect[5].

How Christianity found its way to Carthage
originally must remain uncertain[6]. Some think that
it came by way of Rome, "all roads lead to Rome,"
but many prefer to regard its source as Eastern, and
consider that the undoubted presence of vast numbers
of Jews in the district gives strength to the view that
the Gospel reached North Africa straight from Judaea.
However that may be, we find the Christian community very numerous at Carthage towards the end

[1] Hesterni sumus et vestra omnia implevimus, urbes, insulas,
castella, municipia, conciliabula, castra ipsa, tribus, decurias, pala-
tium, senatum, forum : sola vobis reliquimus templa. Possumus
dinumerare exercitus vestros ; unius provinciae plures erunt. *Apol.*
XXXVII.

[2] Tanta hominum multitudo, pars paene major civitatis cujusque.
ad Scap. II.

[3] Non ulla gens non Christiana. *ad Natt.* I. viii.

[4] Britannorum inaccessa Romanis loca, Christo vero subdita.
adv. Jud. VII.

[5] See Bindley's *Apol.* xxxvii. *note.*

[6] See above, ch. ii. *in.*

of the second century, when Tertullian began his
writings. The passages quoted above from the *Apology* were almost certainly written in the year 197,
perhaps not long after Tertullian's conversion to
Christianity. The treatise itself is possibly the earliest
of his writings—it may have been preceded by the
ad Nationes and *ad Martyras*—and was written in
Latin. And here we may pause to emphasize the
importance of that fact, and to assign to Tertullian the
credit of inventing and perfecting a phraseology in that
language for the purposes of controversy which has
survived ever since, and has been the foundation of all
subsequent developments of ecclesiastical style.

Until Tertullian the only language available had
been Greek: even at Rome in the first century,
S. Paul must have addressed the Church in that
language: all his letters were written in Greek: Greek
in fact was the *lingua franca* for all the civilized world,
and the only recognized medium of communication.
Tertullian is the first author in the Christian Church of
any eminence[1] who wrote in Latin, and he had to
invent many new terms and to employ novel methods
of expression in order to convey to his readers the
new thoughts and ideas with which his own mind was

[1] Of Victor, who was Pope of Rome 189—198 or 199, also a native
of North Africa, who wrote some works in Latin, according to
S. Jerome, see lower, chapter v. p. 125. These have all perished.
The four Latin letters ascribed to him, one of which is addressed *ad
Africanos*, are undoubtedly apocryphal. Cf. Monceaux, p. 54 n.

so fully charged. The style he employs is compressed in the extreme, often crabbed and even uncouth: but there is no doubt that it is forceful and effective.

The *Apology* was called forth by the general attitude of the heathen populace at Carthage towards Christians; it is no meek defence of the Christian position, but a vigorous onslaught into the very heart of heathendom. Tertullian carries the war into the enemy's camp with a vengeance. Hear for instance the vehemence of his invective against idols: "As to your gods, I see merely the names of some old dead folk, and I hear fables about them, and I recognize sacred rites founded on those fables: and as to the idols themselves, I gather nothing else than this; that they are materials akin to the vessels and utensils in common use, or even that they are made of those very same vessels and utensils, as though they could change their destination by being consecrated, transformed by the license accorded to skilled workmanship, and that too in the most outrageous and sacrilegious way in the very act of their transformation; the result is that we who are punished on account of those very gods, can more than other people actually derive consolation in our punishment from the fact that they themselves also suffer in just the same way, in order that they may come into existence at all[1]."

[1] Quantum igitur de Diis vestris, nomina solummodo video quorundam veterum mortuorum, et fabulas audio, et sacra de fabulis recognosco ; quantum autem de simulacris ipsis, nihil aliud depre-

Again, he contrasts the true love among Christians
with its spurious counterfeit to be found among the
heathen: "But even the working of so great a love as
ours merely brands us with a bad mark in the eyes of
some of them. See, they say, how these Christians love
one another: yes, for they themselves only hate one
another : See how ready they are to die for each other :
yes, for they themselves will be found more ready to kill
each other. Further, we recognize one another by the
common name of Brethren ; for this they defame us, for
no other reason I suppose than because amongst themselves there is no name of kinship but what is a sham
and affectation[1]."

He protests vigorously against the readiness to condemn Christians unheard, and says they are so far from
deserving punishment that they ought to be thanked
publicly as the most law-abiding, peaceable, and entirely
praiseworthy part of the population.

The most ridiculous charges, he cries, are brought

hendo, quam materias sorores esse vasculorum instrumentorumque
communium, vel ex iisdem vasculis et instrumentis quasi fatum
consecratione mutantes, licentia artis transfigurante, et quidem con-
tumeliosissime et in ipso opere sacrilege, ut revera nobis maxime,
qui propter deos ipsos plectimur, solatium poenarum esse possit,
quod eadem et ipsi patiuntur, ut fiant. *Apol.* xii.

[1] Sed ejusmodi vel maxime dilectionis operatio notam nobis inurit
penes quosdam. Vide, inquiunt, ut invicem se diligant; qui enim
invicem oderunt : et ut pro alterutro mori sint parati; qui enim ad
occidendum alterutrum paratiores erunt. Sed et quod fratrum
appellatione censemur, non alias, opinor, infamant quam quod apud
ipsos omne sanguinis nomen de affectatione simulatum est. *Apol.*
xxxix.

against them. They are accused of Thyestean orgies, in which they eat the flesh of infant children, followed by nameless revels of bestiality and incest. Ought not men who themselves are guilty of such crimes in the rites of their heathen worship to blush before Christians who are incapable of like excesses[1] ? In short he flings back into the teeth of his opponents far blacker taunts and charges than could possibly be sustained against innocent Christians : persecution he says is an illegality : not only are its victims free from blame, but the evils of paganism are blatant, vile, and known to all : they cannot be concealed or denied : and he goes on to prove that not only is its philosophy futile and helpless, but also the morality inculcated by Christianity is infinitely higher, and its spiritual influence over its votaries most remarkable.

Is there not something essentially modern and familiar in this attitude of mind ? We sympathize with his vigorous outspokenness, his uncompromising straightforwardness, his unfearing denunciations of the lower and his appreciation of the higher ideal : his very combativeness appeals to our Anglo-Saxon instincts, and his fiery invectives still stir our sluggish northern blood, as they come to us across the ages :

---

[1] No doubt this charge so freely brought against Christians, of eating infant flesh and so forth, had its origin in their mysterious allusions to the sacred rites of the Eucharist, the partaking of the Blessed Body and Blood of our Lord.

we have a fellow feeling with his manliness and recognize in him a Leader we could follow.

Space allows the quotation of only one or two more instances of his manner and style: "Oh good presidents," he cries, "go on with your work, sure to be in far better favour with the people, if you sacrifice Christians for them. Torture, rack, condemn, grind us to powder: we raise no objection: for your injustice is the proof of our innocence. Therefore it is that God suffers us to suffer thus. Why, only the other day, when you condemned a Christian woman to the pander rather than the panther you acknowledged that a stain on chastity is considered among us a more awful thing than any punishment or any death. And yet all your cruelty, growing ever more and more refined, profits you not a whit: rather it is an attraction to our sect. The more often we are mown down by you, the more we grow in number: the blood of Christians is the seed (of the Church)......All sins receive pardon in the act (of martyrdom). Hence it is that at the very moment of your pronouncing sentence against us, we give thanks: for as the Divine is the antithesis of the human, so when you condemn us, God acquits us[1]."

[1] Sed hoc agite, boni Praesides, meliores multo apud populum, si illis Christianos immolaveritis. Cruciate, torquete, damnate, atterite nos: probatio est enim innocentiae nostrae iniquitas vestra. Ideo nos haec pati Deus patitur. Nam et proxime, ad lenonem, damnando Christianam potius quam ad leonem, confessi estis labem pudicitiae apud nos atrociorem omni poena et omni morte reputari.

The Theatre, Carthage.

With reference to the Resurrection of the Body, in a passage shortly before the last quotation from the *Apology*, Tertullian answers the objection: " How can matter which has been dissolved be made to appear again ? " by this defence " What were men before they came into existence ? Nothing, you say. What will they be when they cease to exist ? Nothing. Then why might they not come into being again by the will of Him who at first created them out of nothing[1] ? "

In his treatise about the public shows he discusses the question, Should Christians go to the theatre or amphitheatre ? and he answers it emphatically in the negative. Such performances were intimately associated with heathen rites and the worship of idols, and so he urged that the true Christian must have nothing to do with them. He once heard a Christian lover of the games defend his habit of attending them thus: The sun,

Nec quicquam tamen proficit exquisitior quaeque crudelitas vestra : illecebra est magis sectae. Plures efficimur, quotiens metimur a vobis ; semen est sanguis Christianorum...omnia enim huic operi delicta donantur. Inde est, quod ibidem sententiis vestris gratias agimus : ut est aemulatio divinae rei et humanae, cum damnamur a vobis, a Deo absolvimur. *Apol.* L. *sub fin.*

[1] *Apol.* XLVIII. Considera temetipsum, o homo, et fidem rei invenies. Recogita quid fueris antequam esses. Utique nihil. Meminisses, enim, si quid fuisses. Qui ergo nihil fueras priusquam esses, idem nihil factus cum esse desieris, cur non possis rursus esse de nihilo, Ejusdem Ipsius Auctoris voluntate, qui te voluit esse de nihilo? Quid novi tibi eveniet? Qui non eras, factus es ; Cum iterum non eris, fies, &c. Cf. for a similar argument *adv. Hermog.* XX.—XXII. and XXXIV. On these passages see Kaye, p. 536.

he said, nay God Himself looks down from Heaven on the shows, and no contamination follows. Tertullian's retort is crushing : " Yes, and the sun casts his rays into the sewer and is not defiled.".…" Nowhere and never can that be excused which God condemns. Nowhere and never is that lawful which always and everywhere is unlawful[1]." Later on, in the same treatise, he cries, " Oh may God keep from His own this great longing for deadly pleasure ! It is to go from God's Church to the devil's, *de caelo in caenum*, from sky to sty. How can hands raised in prayer to God occupy themselves in clapping the actor ? How can the mouth, which repeats its *Amen* at the reception of the Eucharist, raise an approving shout for the gladiator, or cry ἀπ᾽ αἰῶνος for any but God and Christ[2] ? "

The same uncompromising spirit appears in his treatise *de Corona* : the emperors Severus and Caracalla in 202 had decreed a largess to their soldiery.

---

[1] *de Spect.* xx. Novam proxime defensionem suaviludii cujusdam audivi. Sol, inquit, immo etiam Ipse Deus de caelo spectat, nec contaminatur. Sane Sol et in cloacam radios suos defert, nec inquinatur.…Nusquam et nunquam excusatur quod Deus damnat. Nusquam et nunquam licet quod semper et ubique non licet.

[2] *de Spect.* xxv. Avertat Deus a suis tantam voluptatis exitiosae cupiditatem. Quale est enim de ecclesia Dei in diaboli ecclesiam tendere ? De caelo, quod aiunt, in caenum ? Illas manus, quas ad Deum extuleris, postmodum laudando histrionem fatigare ? Ex ore, quo *Amen* in Sanctum protuleris, gladiatori testimonium reddere, ἀπ᾽ αἰῶνος alii omnino dicere, nisi Deo et Christo ? The translation is Prof. Fuller's, *Dict. Chr. Biogr. s.v.* Tertullianus, p. 831.

This was to be received by them, each wearing the laurel garland, which implied acknowledgment of the emperor's divinity: this a soldier at Carthage, "more the soldier of Christ than of the empire," had re-fused to do, and proclaimed himself a Christian: he was flung into prison and awaited martyrdom. Ter-tullian furiously undertook his defence, and declared that it was impossible for Christians to serve the state as soldiers. Not only so; he even forbids his fellow Christians to take part in ordinary social functions of the day, which can bear any trace whatever of condoning the sin of idolatry; since such met them at every step, he was urging upon them a withdrawal from almost all amenities of social life as well as business pursuits. The ideal seemed unattainable, and it is not surprising that while Christians strongly felt this, the heathen bitterly resented the violence of the attack made upon their most cherished and familiar habits. The result was that to the ordinary citizen of the Empire the Chris-tian seemed an impossible person, a sour ill-conditioned fanatic, a veritable kill-joy, who would join in none of the amusements and relaxations which the conscience of the day considered innocent. It mattered not that the ideal of the Christian was much more right than that of the heathen: the consequence was that the lower orders cordially detested the Christians and rejoiced in their persecution and downfall[1]. Hence followed in

[1] See below, p. 135.

various parts of the empire, and especially in N. Africa, much cruelty and ill usage. This is evident from many passages of Tertullian, and also from the pathetic story of S. Perpetua and S. Felicitas: of which see more below, p. 128 *foll.*

Perhaps the best known instance of Tertullian's epigrammatic style is the oft-quoted passage from *de Carne Christi*, v. "The Son of God was crucified: it shames us not, just because it is shameful. The Son of God died: it is credible, just because it is so absolutely absurd. He was buried and rose again: it is certain, just because it is impossible[1]."

Enough perhaps has now been said to illustrate Tertullian's style and methods of controversy: let us turn once more to the man himself. Between the years 202 and 213 his views underwent a momentous change. His ardent nature had more and more fretted within the bonds of conventionality; he felt that the claims of Christ had been weakened and watered down by the lax tone of society, and the absence of a high moral standard of life: he longed for more austerity, more zealous enthusiasm, a stricter and more literal obedience to Christ's commands. In this frame of mind, he was attracted by the teaching of Montanus and his followers. It is not clear whether Tertullian made acquaintance

---

[1] Crucifixus est Dei Filius: non pudet, quia pudendum est. Et mortuus est Dei Filius: prorsus credibile est, quia ineptum est. Et sepultus resurrexit: certum est, quia impossibile est.

with Montanism at Rome or—as seems more probable—
at Carthage. But the very extravagance of the ideal
demanded for Christian conduct appealed irresistibly to
the African, and by the year 213 he had thrown in his lot
unreservedly with the Montanists. With the same fire
and eloquence, the same caustic wit and biting sarcasm,
with which in earlier days he had flung himself against
the enemies of the Church, he now assailed the Church
itself. For instance in *de Monogamia*, which perhaps
belongs to 217, he claims that the Paraclete reveals to
those spiritually initiated much about marriage which
was not clear in the letter of Holy Scripture, and
characterizes second marriages as adulterous : in *de
Jejunio* he heaps up charges of luxury and gluttony
and immorality unhesitatingly and almost exultingly
against Church ecclesiastics and laymen : they are so
gross as almost to refute themselves by their exaggera-
tion. As Professor Fuller in the *Dict. Christ. Biogr.*
says, " The Ascetic has become a Fanatic, and in his
mad hatred besmirches and calumniates the Church he
had once so tenderly loved."

But it would profit little to dwell on this phase
in his career. His very faults are the result and effect
of his virtues : it is because he is so eagerly jealous to
maintain the highest standard of Christian discipline
and conduct that he cannot have patience with the
easier level of every-day morality, and to his impatience,
more than to any other quality, may be attributed the

want of balance in his judgment. He was keenly conscious of this himself; and there is deep pathos in his words at the opening of *de Patientia* when he admits that Patience is a virtue to which he can lay no claim: "Oh wretched man that I am," he cries, " ever consumed by the fires of Impatience[1]!" The lack of this virtue has led him far from Christ and perhaps deprived him of the title to a saintly life. And yet how we should welcome among us more of his burning zeal for right, his fiery impatience of wrong. We long for the fearless outspokenness, the entire sincerity, the eloquent enthusiasm of a Tertullian, to rouse us from the fatal torpor which paralyses spiritual effort and hinders advance in holiness.

Not without reason did Cyprian, the great bishop of Carthage in the next generation—A.D. 250— proclaim himself Tertullian's humble follower and admirer : every day we are told, however much occupied he might be with distracting and harassing business, he never forgot to study the thoughts of his beloved Teacher. *Da magistrum*, Give me the Master, he used to cry to his secretary[2]. If Cyprian the statesman, the ad-

---

[1] Miserrimus ego, semper aeger caloribus impatientiae !

[2] See Jerome, *de viris illustribus*, LIII. Vidi ego quemdam Paulum Concordiae, quod oppidum Italiae est, senem, qui se Beati Cypriani, jam grandis aetatis, notarium, cum ipse admodum esset adolescens, Romae vidisse diceret, referreque sibi solitum nunquam Cyprianum absque Tertulliani lectione unum diem praeteriisse, ac sibi crebro dicere *Da magistrum*, Tertullianum videlicet significans.

ministrator, the champion of sane and wise Christianity, could feel that he owed so much to Tertullian, is not our own debt equally marked ? Cyprian may well have seen him wandering about the streets of Carthage in extreme old age—Jerome says he lived " usque ad decrepitam aetatem "—and so may be almost termed a late contemporary, who was able to estimate his worth from intimate knowledge. We too looking back across the ages may readily assign to him a foremost place among the Fathers of the Church. Before his sympathies with the extravagances of Montanism had warped his judgment, he had championed the cause of orthodoxy with irresistible force and skill. His tactics and method of stating his case are ingenious, and effective, as we should expect from the trained and subtle lawyer : his personalities, if sometimes lacking in taste, give life and point to his attack. He spares neither the living nor the dead : and so we find him not only the most vigorous but also the most witty and amusing of all theologians.

But he is also among the most earnest and high-minded : before he embraced Montanism, his ideal of the order and discipline of the Church was eminently orthodox, and even spiritual. He regarded the religion of Jesus Christ as the true revelation of God: the religion of the heathen as the service of devils : he had not the same sympathy as the Alexandrian school of apologists, led by Justin Martyr, Clement, and Origen,

with the efforts of non-Christian systems to find God:
with them Christianity was not so much the opponent,
as the evolution of natural philosophy and of Judaism:
to Tertullian "all history, all thought, all religion,
previous to the advent of Christ, was abhorrent:
paganism in every form stood absolutely condemned, as
the rival effort of the opponent of God to enslave the
human intellect and deter it from the knowledge of the
truth[1]." Not only so, but he insists again and again on
the due observance of Church doctrine: he takes his
stand on the Apostolic Creed: if that be admitted, he
is prepared to consider sympathetically and with open
mind wide speculations or theories. On the other hand
he seems to lack due appreciation of the tenderness
and love of Christ, which is a serious defect in his
character: he has much more regard for Him as the
Messiah and the Judge: and this aspect of the Person
of our Lord colours his view of eschatology and Christ's
second coming.

But apart altogether from his particular estimate
of Christianity and his personal character, all his
writings, and especially those which may be classed as
Montanistic, throw a flood of light on the condition of
the Church in the second and early third centuries, and
present to us a picture of how Christians in North
Africa lived and thought and suffered for the faith;

---

[1] Bindley, *Apol.* Intro. p. xix.

and for this we can never be sufficiently grateful. To him above all writers we owe the very existence of ecclesiastical Latin which was the chief medium of proclaiming the Gospel in the West for at least 1300 years: and if some should question his right to be classed among the Saints, yet the great services he has rendered to Christianity, his manly sincerity, and the earnest intensity of his convictions, should go far to entitle him to such a position.

CHAPTER IV

THE CHURCH IN NORTH AFRICA IN TERTULLIAN'S TIME

§ i. *Church Government—The threefold order of Ministry—The position of the Laity.*

IN a well-known passage of the *Apology*, Tertullian draws a picture of the regular gatherings of the Church, in order to convince the Magistrates whom he is addressing, that there is no ground for the charges, so freely brought against the Christians, of undesirable and immoral practices at their meetings. "We are a body," he says, "one in our common religious beliefs, in the unity (*v. l.* divine character) of our discipline, and in the bond of hope. We meet together in an assembly and congregation, in order that we may as it were form a regular body of troops for prayer, and lay siege to God in united supplication. This 'violence[1]' is indeed pleasing to God. We pray too for the emperors, and their ministers, and those in authority under them, for the condition of the world, for general peace, for the

---

[1] Cf. S. Matt. xi. 12 "The Kingdom of Heaven suffereth violence, and the violent take it by force."

delay of final judgment. We meet together for the
public reading of the Holy Scriptures, in case the
present condition of affairs demands any warning or
consideration. In any case, we feed our faith on the
Holy Words, we raise hope, we confirm confidence, we
enforce discipline, by pressing home their precepts: at
the same time also we exhort the faithful, we punish
the guilty, and issue—if need be—the God-given
sentence of excommunication. For judgment is de-
livered with great weight—as with those who are sure
that God's eye is upon them, and that their sentence is
the gravest anticipation of future judgment—in the case
of a man who has sinned in such a way as to be
debarred from sharing in common prayer and the
meetings of the community and all sacred rites. In all
cases, the Presidents are elders of approved character,
who have gained the office not by bribery but by general
recognition : nor indeed can anything pertaining to God
be associated with bribery. Moreover, if there be any kind
of common fund, the collection is not made with money
paid under a sense of obligation, as though religion could
be bought : everyone puts by a small sum on a certain
day every month, or when he likes, and if he likes, and if
he can : for no one is obliged to do so : the contribution
is voluntary. These are as it were the pledges of piety:
for with them no payment is made for banquets, or
drinking bouts, or disgraceful orgies, but for the support and burial of the poor, for destitute and orphaned

boys and girls, for old men who cannot go out to work, for shipwrecked sailors, and any who, in the mines and islands or prisons, have to suffer for their confession, provided it be on account of God's religion[1]."

[1] Corpus sumus de conscientia religionis et disciplinae unitate (*v. l.* divinitate) et spei foedere. Coimus in coetum et congregationem, ut ad Deum quasi manu facta precationibus ambiamus orantes: haec vis Deo grata est. Oramus etiam pro imperatoribus, pro ministris eorum et potestatibus, pro statu saeculi, pro rerum quiete, pro mora finis. Coimus ad litterarum divinarum commemorationem, si quid praesentium temporum qualitas aut praemonere cogit aut recognoscere. Certe fidem sanctis vocibus pascimus, spem erigimus, fiduciam figimus, disciplinam praeceptorum nihilominus inculcationibus densamus : ibidem etiam exhortationes, castigationes, et censura divina : nam et judicatur magno cum pondere, ut apud certos de Dei conspectu, sum-mumque futuri judicii praejudicium est, si quis ita deliquerit ut a communicatione orationis et conventus et omnis sancti commercii relegetur. Praesident probati quique seniores, honorem istum non pretio sed testimonio adepti : neque enim pretio ulla res Dei constat. Etiam si quod arcae genus est, non de honoraria summa quasi redemp-tae religionis congregatur. Modicam unusquisque stipem menstrua die, vel cum velit, et si modo velit, et si modo possit, apponit; nam nemo compellitur, sed sponte confert. Haec quasi deposita pietatis sunt. Nam inde non epulis nec potaculis nec ingratiis voratrinis dispensatur, sed egenis alendis humandisque, et pueris ac puellis re ac parentibus destitutis, jamque domesticis senibus, item naufragis, et si qui in metallis, et si qui in insulis vel in custodiis, dumtaxat ex causa Dei sectae, alumni confessionis suae fiunt. *Apol.* xxxix.

The familiar description by Justin Martyr (*Apol.* LXVII.) of the Christian Sunday service aptly illustrates this passage : it belongs to a date earlier by some 40 years and is quoted in full by Oehler *ad loc.*, "on the day of the week called Sunday, all who live in the cities or country round gather together at the same place, and the memorials of the Apostles or the writings of the Prophets are read aloud as long as there is time ; then when the reader ceases, the President by word of mouth

In this passage Tertullian does not enter into the details of Church government, as he is addressing a heathen audience : but the " Presidents " of whom he speaks must include both Bishops and Priests. This is evident from several passages : *e.g.* " We receive (the elements in the Eucharist) from the hand of no one but the Presidents[1]." This would mean primarily the Bishop, who presided at the Holy Eucharist: but in his absence the Presbyter would officiate. The same is implied in *ad ux.* I. vii. when compared with 1 Tim. iii. 2 and Tit. i. 6. " The discipline of the Church and the directions of the Apostle, which forbid those who have married twice to be Presidents, sufficiently shew what a loss to the Faith and what an obstacle to holiness

---

makes his exhortation and appeal to all to imitate so good a pattern. Then we rise all together and pray: and as I said before, when we have finished our prayers, there is an oblation of bread, and wine and water. Then the President offers prayers and thanksgivings alike, to the best of his ability, and the people answer ' Amen ' : and the Eucharistic offerings are distributed and received by all present, and sent to those who are absent by the hand of the Deacons."

[1] Nec de aliorum manu quam Praesidentium sumimus. *de Cor.* III. In another passage he laments that sometimes these Presidents are engaged in the trade of the manufacture of idols: it is not enough (he says) that idol-makers defile the body of the Lord by receiving it into their contaminated hands : idol-makers are actually admitted into Holy Orders. Parum sit, si ab aliis manibus accipiant quod contaminant, sed etiam ipsae tradunt aliis quod contaminaverunt. Adleguntur in ordinem ecclesiasticum artifices idolorum. Pro scelus ! Semel Judaei Christo manus intulerunt, isti quotidie corpus Ejus lacessunt. *de Idol.* VII.

second marriages are[1]." In a later passage written
from the extreme Montanist point of view, he implies
that the Orthodox Church (*Psychici*) limit the "double
honour" to be paid (according to 1 Tim. v. 17 to οἱ
καλῶς προεστῶτες πρεσβύτεροι) to Priests and Bishops,
whereas it is due to "the brethren as well as to those
set over them[2]." This "double honour" he seems
strangely to interpret as meaning a double portion of
food.

We find the three orders of Bishops, Priests and
Deacons specifically named more than once : *e.g.* in
de fuga in persecutione, XI. he pleads for courage on the
part of Church leaders, and says, "When even the leaders
of the Church, that is even the Deacons, Presbyters and
Bishops, take to flight, how will the Laity be able to
understand the meaning of the saying, Flee ye from
state to state ? So when generals flee, &c.[3]"

In discussing by whose hands Baptism may be
administered, he says, "The chief Priest who is the
Bishop has the right of administering (Baptism). Then
the Presbyters and Deacons, not however without

---

[1] Quantum detrahant Fidei, quantum obstrepant sanctitati
nuptiae secundae, disciplina ecclesiae et praescriptio Apostoli declarat,
quum digamos non sinit praesidere.

[2] Ad elogium gulae tuae pertinet, quod duplex apud te praesidenti-
bus honor binis partibus deputatur, cum apostolus duplicem honorem
dederit, ut et fratribus et praepositis.   *de jejun. adv. Psych.* XVII.

[3] Cum ipsi auctores, id est Diaconi et Presbyteri et Episcopi
fugiunt, quomodo laicus intelligere poterit qua ratione dictum, Fugite
de civitate in civitatem ?   Itaque cum duces fugiunt, &c.

authority from the Bishop, for the honour of the Church: if that be ensured, peace is ensured: on other occasions also Lay folk possess the right¹."

The same distinction is made in the passage where he speaks of the dangers of indiscipline among heretics: "And so to-day one man is Bishop, to-morrow another: to-day he is Deacon, who to-morrow is Reader : to-day he is Presbyter who to-morrow is a Layman : for to the Laity also they assign priestly functions²." From these words it follows that the orthodox Church recognized a clear distinction between Clergy and Laity. Tertullian even states that different seats were assigned to them in the places where they assembled for divine worship. "The authority of the Church has ordained a difference between those in Holy Orders and the Laity; and respect is paid to their sacred office by the special seats of the clergy³." The same fact appears from his dividing Christians into two classes, those with a lower and those with a higher place : every servant

¹ Dandi quidem habet jus summus sacerdos, qui est Episcopus : dehinc Presbyteri et Diaconi, non tamen sine Episcopi auctoritate, propter ecclesiae honorem, quo salvo salva pax est. Alioquin etiam Laicis jus est: &c. *de Baptismo*, xvii.—on this point see lower, the section on Baptism, p. 61 *foll.*

² Itaque alius hodie Episcopus, cras alius: hodie Diaconus qui cras Lector: hodie Presbyter qui cras Laicus: nam et Laicis sacerdotalia munera injungunt. *de Praescr. Haeret.* xli.

³ Differentiam inter ordinem et plebem constituit ecclesiae auctoritas, et honor per ordinis consessum sanctificatus. *de Exhort. Castit.* vii. See above, pp. 18, 19.

of God, he says, should try to rise from one to the other by enduring persecution; and in the next sentence he mentions "Deacons, Priests and Bishops[1]." In another passage, he distinctly calls the ordained Clergy—Bishops, Priests and Deacons—*majores* as contrasted with the Laity[2].

Later on in the passage from *de Exhort. Cast.* VII. just quoted, he argues thus: "As a general rule, the Sacraments of Baptism and the Holy Eucharist can only be administered by the ordained clergy: in cases of necessity, where no clergy are available, a Layman may officiate: inasmuch therefore as a Priest is not allowed to contract a second marriage—if he does, he is *ipso facto* deprived of his priestly functions—a Layman also should avoid taking a second wife, in order that he may be free to administer the Sacraments should necessity arise[3]."

[1] Hoc sentire et facere omnem servum Dei oportet, etiam minoris loci, ut majoris fieri possit, si quem gradum in persecutionis toler-antia ascenderit. *de fuga in persec.* XI. followed by the quotation given above.

[2] Quanto magis Laicis disciplina verecundiae et modestiae incum-bit, cum ea *majoribus* competant. *de Bapt.* XVII.

[3] Ubi ecclesiastici Ordinis non est consessus, et offers (*i.e.* celebrate the Eucharist) et tinguis (*i.e.* baptize) et sacerdos es tibi solus...igitur si habes jus sacerdotis in temetipso ubi necesse est, habeas oportet etiam disciplinam sacerdotis, ubi necesse sit habere jus sacerdotis. Digamus tinguis? Digamus offers? Quanto magis laico digamo capitale est agere pro sacerdote, quum ipsi sacerdoti digamo facto auferatur agere sacerdotem!...Noli denique digamus deprehendi, et non committis in necessitatem administrandi quod non licet digamo. *de Exh. Cast.* VII.

Enough has been said to shew that Tertullian—
though as a Montanist he receded later from the
position—asserts that the orthodox Church clearly
recognized the distinction between Clergy and Laity.
But he is not so clear as to the distinction in pre-
rogatives and position between the Bishop and the
Presbyter. His Montanistic sympathies seem to have
asserted themselves early, and for him tended eventually to merge the one office into the other. Nevertheless, it is clear throughout that the Bishop is the
supreme officer, and the source of highest authority.
In a passage in *de Praescr. Haer.* he traces the origin of
the Church back to the preaching of the twelve Apostles
(Matthias taking the place of the traitor Judas) first in
Judaea, and then through all the world. He will not
acknowledge the authority of a Church which cannot
prove its Apostolic origin[1]; and it is not too much to
say that he thereby accepts the doctrine of Apostolic
succession in the persons of those who presided over the
various Churches, *i.e.* the Bishops, who were appointed
one after the other in succession to the Apostles themselves, the original founders of the Churches[2].

[1] Cf. *de Virg. vel.* II. Eas ego ecclesias proposui quas et ipsi
Apostoli vel Apostolici viri condiderunt.

[2] Apostoli...primo per Judaeam contestata fide in Jesum Christum
et ecclesiis institutis, dehinc in orbem profecti eandem doctrinam
ejusdem fidei nationibus promulgaverunt. Et perinde ecclesias apud
unamquamque civitatem condiderunt, a quibus traducem fidei et
semina doctrinae ceterae exinde ecclesiae mutuatae sunt, et cotidie
mutuantur, ut ecclesiae fiant, ac per hoc et ipsae apostolicae deputa-
buntur ut suboles apostolicarum ecclesiarum. *de Praescr. Haer.* xx.

The same is implied in a later passage of the same Tract, where Tertullian challenges heretics to produce such claim for authority as can be shewn for instance by the Churches of Smyrna and Rome. "Let them shew," he says, "the origin of their Churches; let them trace the order of their Bishops, following one another in succession from the very first in such a way as to prove that their first Bishop had for his teacher and predecessor one of the Apostles or some Apostolic man who always continued faithful to Apostolic teaching. For it is in this way that the Apostolic Churches shew their origin, just as the Church of the people of Smyrna goes back to Polycarp who was placed there by John, and that of the Romans in the same way to Clement who was ordained by Peter[1]."

Herein rests the claim for the unity of the Church: the various Churches, provided they be Apostolic, are all branches of the true Church, equal in rank and authority, and independent of one another; and although they severally may fall into error[2] yet taken together the unity of the whole Church is not impaired.

---

[1] Edant ergo origines ecclesiarum suarum, evolvant ordinem episcoporum suorum, ita per successionem ab initio decurrentem, ut primus ille episcopus aliquem ex apostolis vel apostolicis viris, qui tamen cum apostolis perseveravit, habuerit auctorem et antecessorem. Hoc enim modo ecclesiae apostolicae census suos deferunt, sicut Smyrnaeorum ecclesia Polycarpum ab Joanne collocatum refert, sicut Romanorum Clementem a Petro ordinatum itidem. *de Praescr. Haer.* xxxii.

[2] This is explicitly stated in *de Praescr. Haer.* xxvii.

So Tertullian expressly asserts : "We and they (*i.e.*
Apostolic Churches with customs differing from our
own) have one Faith, one God, the same Christ, the
same Hope, the same rites of Baptism: once for
all I would say, we are one Church[1]." And again,
"Though the Churches be so many and so important,
yet all are one : they are the first Church founded by
the Apostles, from which all the rest come[2]."

Although from the words of S. Cyprian[3] we may
conclude that there were synods or councils of the
Church in North Africa, soon after, if not actually
during Tertullian's time, he himself does not give us
any clear information on the matter. In one passage
he speaks of " councils of all the Churches, by means
of which matters of the highest importance are discussed in common, and themselves are representative
of all who bear the name of Christ and are held in
highest respect," but he refers to them only in connexion with certain places where the Greek language
is spoken[4]. In another passage he implies that councils

[1] Una nobis et illis Fides, unus Deus, idem Christus, eadem spes,
eadem lavacri sacramenta ; semel dixerim, Una ecclesia sumus. *de
Virg. vel.* II.

[2] Tot ac tantae ecclesiae una est illa ab Apostolis prima, ex qua
omnes. *de Praescr. Haer.* XX.

[3] See above, p. 26.

[4] Aguntur praeterea per Graecias illa certis in locis concilia
ex universis ecclesiis per quae et altiora quaeque in commune tractan-
tur, et ipsa repraesentatio totius nominis Christiani magna veneratione
celebratur. *de jejun. adv. Psych.* XIII.

had much to do with settling the Canon of Scripture, for he says that the *Shepherd of Hermas* was counted among apocryphal and false books even by councils of the orthodox Church[1]. But he nowhere speaks expressly of synods of the Church in North Africa.

Of the many African Bishops who must have been Tertullian's contemporaries, the names of only two survive: *viz.* Optatus, who is named in the Passion of S. Perpetua[2], and Agrippinus, who is mentioned by S. Cyprian as presiding over a council of the African Church about the rebaptism of heretics " very many years before his time[3]." This passage may—and probably does—imply that there were councils of North African Bishops during Tertullian's lifetime, though he does not say so himself.

It is perhaps worth notice that the title *Papa* is used in the Passion of S. Perpetua of the Bishop, and is also applied by Tertullian to the Bishop of Rome, Pope Callistus, of whom he speaks ironically as " the good shepherd and blessed Pope[4]."

---

[1] Sed cederem tibi, si Scriptura Pastoris, quae sola moechos amat, divino instrumento meruisset incidi, si non ab omni concilio ecclesiarum, etiam vestrarum, inter apocrypha et falsa judicaretur. *de Pudic.* x.   [2] See p. 133.

[3] Cypr. *Ep.* LXXIII. 3. Apud nos autem non mora et repentina res est ut baptizandos censeamus eos qui ab haereticis ad ecclesiam veniunt : quando anni sint jam multi et longa aetas ex quo sub Agrippino convenientes in unum episcopi plurimi hoc statuerint.

[4] Bonus Pastor et benedictus Papa, *de Pudic.* XIII. : but Münter, followed by Oehler, refers this to the Bishop of Carthage.

Besides the ordinary Clergy, Bishops, Priests and Deacons, Tertullian recognizes also an order of "Readers[1]"
and of "Widows[2]": but he does not specifically name
the order of Deaconesses.

As to the Laity, in one passage he sums them all
up under the term "Learners" or "Disciples[3]." "If
there be no Bishop, or Priests, or Deacons, ordinary
Disciples are sent for," *i.e.* to administer Baptism.
To them different titles are given according to their
progress or position in the Faith: before Baptism, they
are *catechumeni, audientes, auditores, novitioli*[4]; after
Baptism they are ranked as *Fratres*, "Brethren,"
Fideles, "the Faithful," Confessors, Martyrs: titles ap-
plicable also on occasion even before Baptism[5]. He
finds fault with heretics for making no distinction
between those under instruction and the duly baptized
members of the Church[6].

In the actual direction of Church government the

[1] *de Praescr. Haeret.* XLI. quoted above, p. 47.

[2] *de virg. vel.* IX., *de monog.* XVI. and *de Exh. Cast.* XII. and other
passages.

[3] Nisi Episcopus jam aut Presbyteri aut Diaconi, vocantur discentes. *de Bapt.* XVII. On this passage see below, § ii. p. 61.

[4] *de Paen.* VI. an alius est intinctis Christus, alius audientibus?
...audientes optare intinctionem, non praesumere oportet, &c.

[5] This appears from a passage in *de Cor.* II. Neminem dico Fidelium
coronam capite nosse alias extra tempus temptationis ejusmodi:
omnes ita observant, a catechumenis usque ad confessores et
martyres.

[6] Quis catechumenus, quis Fidelis incertum est...ante sunt per-
fecti catechumeni quam edocti. *de Praescr. Haer.* XLI.

Laity had no small share. As soon as they were baptized they had a voice in all that concerned the welfare of the community, and they retained this unless they were excommunicated, or relegated to the ranks of Penitents, owing to gross sin or breach of discipline. They had the right of assisting in the choice of all their clergy, even of the Bishop. By the time of S. Cyprian this intervention of the Laity in Church politics and government had become constant, and even led to some difficulties: a fact which may be inferred also from the words of Tertullian already alluded to, in *de Bapt.* XVII., where he is saying that Baptism may be administered by Laymen, but only in cases of necessity. "But inasmuch as these privileges—of administering the Sacraments, &c.—belong to their superiors, all the more is the duty of modesty and self-control incumbent on the Laity, so as to prevent their arrogating to themselves duties belonging to the Bishop. It is jealousy of the episcopate which is the fruitful source—the mother—of schisms[1]."

§ ii. *Baptism.*

In his treatise *de Baptismo*, Tertullian emphasizes the paramount necessity of Baptism by water from the

---

[1] Sed quanto magis Laicis disciplina verecundiae et modestiae incumbit, cum ea majoribus competant, ne sibi adsumant dicatum episcopi officium. Episcopatus aemulatio schismatum mater est.

quaint conceit that "we, the little fishes of Jesus Christ our ΙΧΘΥΣ[1], are born in the water and can only live by remaining in it: and so that most monstrous (viper of the Caian heresy)[2]...knew very well that it kills the little fishes by taking them away from the water[3]."

In the same treatise, all details of this Sacrament are described at length. He begins by a few remarks on the simplicity of the rite as contrasted with the eternity of its results. "There is nothing which hardens men's hearts so much as the simplicity of God's working as actually seen when compared with the magnificent splendour of its results: take the case of Baptism: in all simpleness, without any pomp or show, indeed without any outlay at all, a man is plunged into water and with the addition of a few words he is baptized: he comes up again no whit cleaner or very little, and yet is the possessor of Eternal Life: this seems a thing incredible to some....Shame on your incredulity which denies to God His own attributes of simplicity and power. What, you say, is it not a marvellous thing that Death should be destroyed by a bath? Nay, it becomes all the more

---

[1] sc. Ἰησοῦς Χριστὸς Θεοῦ Υἱὸς Σωτήρ.

[2] The reading is uncertain: cf. Lupton's Edition of the de Bapt. p. xiv.

[3] Nos pisciculi secundum ΙΧΘΥΝ nostrum Jesum Christum in aqua nascimur, nec aliter quam in aqua permanendo salvi sumus. Itaque illa monstrosissima (de Gaiana heresi Vipera)...optime norat pisciculos necare de aqua auferens. de Baptismo, i.

worthy of belief, if just because it is marvellous it is
therefore not believed[1]."

The formal renunciation of the Devil and all his
works is not expressly mentioned in this passage,
because it did not form part of the actual rite but
preceded it, as will appear directly. The *pauca
verba* of the officiating minister is obviously the form of
Baptism into the Threefold name, in accordance with the
commands of Christ (Matt. xxviii. 19). That this is the
case is shewn by a later passage in this same treatise,
where, after likening the angel of Baptism to the
angel who stirred the water in the pool of Bethesda[2]—
owing to the fact that the latter healed men's bodies,
while the former heals men's souls—he goes on to
compare the rite of Baptism, as the preparation for the
gift of the Holy Spirit, to S. John Baptist the forerunner
of Christ: and incidentally takes it for granted that
Baptism is in the name of the Trinity: "John went
before the Lord, to prepare His ways. So also the angel

[1] *de Bapt.* ii. Nihil adeo est quod obduret mentes hominum
quam simplicitas divinorum operum quae in actu videntur, et magni-
ficentia quae in effectu repromittitur: ut hinc quoque, quoniam tanta
simplicitate, sine pompa, sine apparatu novo aliquo, denique sine
sumptu homo in aqua demissus et inter pauca verba tinctus non
multo vel nihilo mundior resurgit, eo incredibilis existimetur consecutio aeternitatis.... Pro misera incredulitas, quae denegas Deo
proprietates suas, simplicitatem et potestatem! Quid ergo? Nonne
mirandum et lavacro dilui mortem? Atquin eo magis credendum, si
quia mirandum est, idcirco non creditur. Observe that in this passage
and also in that next quoted we have the doctrine of Baptismal
Regeneration explicitly asserted.

[2] Joh. v. 2, 4; he calls it *piscina Bethsaida.* (*de Bapt.* v.)

who presides over the rite of Baptism makes straight
the ways for the on-coming Holy Spirit by the washing
away of sins, which Faith gains by being signed (with
the cross) in the name of the Father and of the Son
and of the Holy Spirit[1]."

Then follows the rite of unction : " On leaving the
font," he says, " we are anointed with the Holy Oil,
according to the ancient custom," sc. of the Jews[2].

After this comes—a sequence which is still observed
in the Greek Church—the rite of Confirmation by the
laying on of hands. " Then follows the laying on of
hands, invoking and inviting the Holy Spirit by way of
benediction[3]."

Thus the order of the actual service in the rite of
Baptism was (1) the immersion, (2) unction, (3) the
signing of the Cross, (4) the laying on of hands, and
apparently, (5) the reception of the Holy Communion
as is summarized in de Resur. Car. VIII.[4]   Tertullian

---

[1] de Bapt. VI. Joannes ante praecursor Domini fuit, praeparans
vias Ejus. Ita et angelus baptismi arbiter superventuro Spiritui
Sancto vias dirigit ablutione delictorum, quam fides impetrat obsig-
nata in Patre et Filio et Spiritui Sancto. Cf. adv. Prax. XXVI. " Not
once but thrice are we baptized, into the name of Each Person (of the
Blessed Trinity) separately."   Nam nec semel, sed ter, ad singula
nomina in personas singulas tingimur.

[2] Exinde egressi de lavacro perungimur benedicta unctione de
pristina disciplina, qua ungi oleo de cornu in sacerdotio solebant.
ibid. VII.

[3] ibid. VIII. Dehinc manus imponitur, per benedictionem advo-
cans et invitans Spiritum Sanctum.

[4] Caro abluitur, ut anima emaculetur; caro ungitur, ut anima

also in another passage sums up the spiritual results of
Baptism under four heads, *viz.* Forgiveness of Sins,
Deliverance from Death, Regeneration, the Gift of the
Holy Spirit[1].

Tertullian on the whole advises against infant
Baptism. "It is better to delay baptism, especially in
the case of infants. Why run the risk of unfaithful
sponsors[2]? Why should the innocent age of child-
hood be in a hurry to obtain forgiveness of sins[3]?"

The rite is summarily described in *de Corona*, III.
where he is insisting on the force of custom and tradition as complementary to the authority of Holy
Scripture. "Those of us who are to be baptized, at
the same time but a little while beforehand, under the
direction of the President, in church (*i.e.* in the place
of assembly[4]) publicly renounce the Devil and his
pomp and his angels. Then we are immersed thrice

---

consecretur; caro signatur, ut et anima muniatur; caro manus
impositione adumbratur, ut et anima spiritu illuminetur: caro
corpore et sanguine Christi vescitur, ut et anima de Deo saginetur.

[1] *adv. Marc.* I. xxviii. Remissio delictorum—absolutio mortis—
regeneratio hominis—consecutio Spiritus Sancti.

[2] In *de Bapt.* VI. Tertullian implies that the number of sponsors at Baptism is three. Cum sub tribus et testatio fidei et *sponsio
salutis* pignerentur, &c.

[3] *de Baptismo*, XVIII. ...Cunctatio baptismi utilior est, praecipue
tamen circa parvulos. Quid enim necesse (si non tam necesse est)
sponsores etiam periculo ingeri, qui et ipsi per mortalitatem destituere
promissiones suas possunt et proventu malae indolis falli?...Quid
festinat innocens aetas ad remissionem peccatorum?

[4] *de Bap.* XIII. Ipsum curiae nomen ecclesia est Christi.

with a somewhat fuller formula than that laid down in the Gospel by our Lord. Then we partake of a mixture of milk and honey, and from that day for a whole week refrain from our daily bath[1]."

The formal renunciation of the Devil and all his works was made before the actual rite of Baptism, as appears from the following passage: "On entering the water we profess the Christian Faith according to the words of His own Law, we publicly declare with our own lips that we renounce the Devil and his pomp and his angels[2]." This seems to have been done twice, *first* during the previous preparation of the catechumen, and *secondly*, just before the actual service: "We... have twice renounced idols," he says[3].

The passage in *de Cor.* III. is markedly in accordance with the Canons of Hippolytus xxix. 102 *seq.*[4], which give us, as many think, the ritual of the order of

[1] Ut a baptismate ingrediar—aquam adituri ibidem, sed et aliquanto prius, in ecclesia sub antistitis manu contestamur nos renuntiare diabolo et pompae et angelis ejus. Dehinc ter mergitamur amplius aliquid respondentes quam Dominus in Evangelio determinavit. Inde suscepti lactis et mellis concordiam praegustamus exque ea die lavacro quotidiano per totam hebdomadem abstinemus.

[2] Cum aquam ingressi Christianam fidem in legis suae verba profitemur, renuntiasse nos diabolo et pompae et angelis ejus ore nostro contestamur. *de Spect.* IV. So also *ib.* XIII., XXIV.

[3] Nobis, qui bis idolis renuntiavimus. *de Spect.* XIII. In a later passage of the same treatise we read "The pomp of the Devil, which we abjure in our baptism." Pompa Diaboli, adversus quam in signaculo fidei ejeramus. *de Spect.* XXIV.

[4] See d'Alès, p. 335.

Baptism as practised in the Church of Rome about the year 200 A.D. There, the preliminary is the examination of the candidate and his confession, followed by his public renunciation of the Devil and all his works, and his declaration of faith in the Trinity; thereafter he receives the triple immersion, and partakes of milk and honey, food symbolical of the life renewed in Christ.

There is no ground for supposing, as some have inferred from *de Pud.* IX.[1], that the bestowal of a ring formed part of the ceremony of Baptism. In that passage Tertullian is commenting on the parable of the Prodigal Son, and in interpreting Luc. xv. 22, he remarks that the ring which the Father bids the servant put on his son's finger is "the mark of Baptism," or answers to Baptism : not that it was used in Baptism as a general rule. No trace of such a custom is to be found elsewhere.

Tertullian is clear that Baptism by Heretics is invalid and cannot be recognized : it does not exist, and so it is not a thing which can be received[2]. He goes on to say that he has dealt with this subject more fully in a Greek treatise, no longer extant. His disciple

---

[1] Anulum—signaculum lavacri : and again, anulum quoque accepit tunc primum, quo fidei pactionem interrogatus obsignat.

[2] Nec baptismus unus, quia non idem ; quem cum rite non habeant, sine dubio non habent, nec capit numerari quod non habetur : Ita nec possunt accipere, quia non habent. *de Bapt.* xv.

and admirer S. Cyprian speaks even more unreservedly : "We say that those who come to us from heretical churches are not *re*baptized by us, but baptized : for indeed they cannot as heretics receive something (by baptism) where nothing exists[1]." Tertullian makes the same statement in what is perhaps his latest treatise, from the Montanistic point of view: "a heretic," he says, "is regarded by us in the same category as a heathen man, yes and something more than a heathen : he is admitted into the Church by the Baptism of Truth, so receiving purification under both heads," *i.e.* both as a heretic and a heathen[2].

Baptism in case of need is to be administered by any member of the Church. "Otherwise (*i.e.* apart from the authority of the Bishop), even the laity have the right (of baptizing). For what is received equally (by all) can be given equally (by all). If no Bishops or Priests or Deacons are available, Disciples (*i.e.* Laymen) are summoned (*i.e.* to baptize[3]). The word of the Lord ought not to be hidden from anyone. So Baptism too,

---

[1] Nos autem dicimus eos qui inde veniunt non rebaptizari apud nos, sed baptizari. Neque enim accipiunt illic aliquid ubi nihil est : quoted by Oehler (from Rigault) *ad loc.*

[2] Apud nos, ut Ethnico par, immo et super Ethnicum, Haereticus etiam per baptisma veritatis utroque nomine purgatus admittitur. *de Pudic.* xix.

[3] Bishop Kaye p. 420 reads *vocarentur* and gives a different explanation to these words. Waterland reads *vocantur dicentes.* Lupton reads *vocantur discentes*, but his rendering of the words seems to me improbable.

equally divine property, can be administered by all[1] ";
i.e. "the Word and Sacraments, since they equally
belong to God, are equally free to all."

But, he goes on, With what care and circumspection
should this assumption of office be exercised[2]. "Since
the duty of administering the sacraments belongs to
their superiors, how much more incumbent on the
Laity is the discipline of modesty and moderation, so
as to prevent their taking upon themselves the consecrated office of Bishop! Jealousy of the episcopate is
the mother of schisms. All things are lawful, said the
most holy Apostle, but not all things are expedient[3].
Let it suffice, that is to say, for you to exercise the
functions (of Bishop) in cases of necessity, if ever
conditions of place or time or person compel you to do
so, but not otherwise[4]."

---

[1] *de Bapt.* xvii. Alioquin etiam laicis jus est. Quod enim ex
aequo accipitur, ex aequo dari potest. Nisi episcopi jam aut Presbyteri aut Diaconi, vocantur Discentes. Domini sermo non debet abscondi
ab ullo. Proinde et baptismus, aeque Dei census, ab omnibus exerceri
potest. Lupton in his edition of the *de Baptismo* (Camb. Patristic
Texts, 1908) translates *aeque Dei census* = "which is equally derived
from God."

[2] Already quoted above, see ch. iv. § i. *sub fin.* p. 54.

[3] 1 Cor. vi. 12 : x. 23.

[4] *ibid.* xvii. Sed quanto magis laicis disciplina verecundiae et
modestiae incumbit, cum ea majoribus competant, ne sibi adsumant
dicatum episcopi officium! episcopatus aemulatio schismatum mater
est. Omnia licere dixit sanctissimus Apostolus, sed non omnia
expedire. Sufficiat scilicet in necessitatibus ut utaris, sicubi aut loci
aut temporis aut personae conditio compellit.

The statement " Baptism may be administered by all[1] " would seem to include women: but this is strongly deprecated in the ensuing words of this chapter ; nor will Tertullian allow any weight to the apocryphal "Acts of Paul and Thecla," which defend the custom : If women are not allowed even to speak in the churches[2] how much less to baptize ?   The same parallel is made in *de Virg. Vel.* IX. "It is not permitted unto women to speak in church, and so neither to teach, nor to baptize, nor to celebrate the Eucharist, nor to claim for themselves the performance of any of man's duties, far less sacerdotal functions[3]."

It is brought as a reproach against women belonging to heretical sects that they even venture to baptize : " The very women of Heretics, how wanton they are ! for they dare to teach...perhaps even to baptize[4]."

The doctrine of Baptismal Regeneration is clearly enunciated at the beginning of the treatise *de Baptismo* I., " Happy is the Sacrament of Baptism : for by the washing away of the sins of our former blindness we are set free for Life Eternal[5]."

[1] *ibid.* Baptismus ab omnibus exerceri potest.

[2] 1 Cor. xiv. 34.

[3] Non permittitur mulieri in ecclesia loqui, sed nec docere nec tingere nec offerre, nec ullius virilis muneris, nedum sacerdotalis officii, sortem sibi vindicare.

[4] Ipsae mulieres haereticae quam procaces ! quae audeant docere... forsitan et tingere.   *de Praescr. Haeret.* XLI.

[5] Felix sacramentum aquae nostrae, quia ablutis delictis pristinae caecitatis in vitam aeternam liberamur.   *Cf.* also p. 56 n.

This belief naturally led many to postpone their Baptism till they were at the point of death, so as to enter into the presence of God clean and white : but the practice receives no countenance from Tertullian. He would have Catechumens baptized on reaching years of discretion, after careful preparation and examination : and then, being in a state of grace, they must sin no more[1].

His three treatises on Baptism, on the Lord's Prayer, and on Penitence, were evidently composed primarily for the use of Catechumens, and belong to the years 200—206, before the severity of Montanism had completely warped his judgment.

In *de Bapt.* XIX. he names Good Friday as the most suitable day for Baptism, "when also the Passion of the Lord into which we are baptized was fulfilled[2]." In support of this practice he quaintly reminds us that when Christ sent forward His Disciples to make preparations for His Last Supper, He said, "You will meet a man bearing a pitcher of *water*[3]." "From Easter to Pentecost," he goes on to say, "is the happiest interval for the administration of Baptism, during which not only was the Lord's Resurrection their constant theme among the Disciples, but also

[1] See below, § vi. on Penance, p. 88 *foll.*

[2] Diem baptismo sollemniorem Pascha praestat, cum et Passio Domini in qua tingimur adimpleta est. Cf. Rom. vi. 3, 4—see the Bp of Salisbury, *Ministry of Grace*, p. 355.

[3] Mk xiv. 3.

there was the consecration of the grace of the Holy
Spirit, and the hope of the Lord's coming was set
forth, because at that moment when He was received
into heaven the angels said to the Apostles[1] that He
should so come in like manner as He ascended into
Heaven, that is to say on the Day of Pentecost[2]."
"But," he after all concludes, "every day is the Lord's,
every hour, every time is suitable for baptism: if there
is an advantage by way of solemnity, there is no
difference so far as grace is concerned[3]."

Before Baptism must come earnest prayer, fasting,
vigils, and confession[4]. So "we set up bulwarks against
ensuing temptations[5]." He reminds his Catechumens
that the Lord Himself had to go straight from his
Baptism to His 40 days' fast and to be tempted by the
Devil, shewing us that man does not " live by the Bread

---

[1] Acts i. 11. Tertullian therefore interprets this passage as referring to the descent of the Holy Spirit at Pentecost, rather than to
Christ's second coming to judge the world.

[2] Exinde Pentecoste ordinandis lavacris laetissimum spatium est,
quo et Domini resurrectio inter discipulos frequentata est, et gratia
Spiritus Sancti dedicata, et spes adventus Domini subostensa, quod
tunc in caelos recuperato Eo angeli ad apostolos dixerunt sic venturum,
quemadmodum et in caelos conscendit, utique in Pentecoste.

[3] ibid. Ceterum omnis dies Domini est, omnis hora, omne tempus
habile baptismo : si de sollemnitate interest, de gratia nihil refert.

[4] de Bapt. xx. Ingressuros baptismum orationibus crebris, jejuniis
et geniculationibus et pervigiliis orare oportet et cum confessione
omnium retro delictorum.

[5] ibid. Subsecuturis tentationibus munimenta praestruimus.

of God but by the Word of God[1]," and he concludes with this touching and eloquent address to those whom he has been preparing for baptism : "Therefore, Blessed (children), for whom the grace of God is waiting, when ye come up out of that most holy font of the New Birth, and for the first time in the house of your mother —the Church—in company with your brethren stretch out open hands in prayer, ask from your Father, ask from the Lord, peculiar gifts of grace ; ask that special marks of Divine Favour may be distributed among you. Ask and ye shall receive, He says[2]. Ye indeed have sought, and ye have found : ye have knocked and it has been opened unto you. This only I beg, that when ye are asking, ye do not forget to pray also for Tertullian the sinner[3]."

§ iii. *The Agape or Love Feast.*

In Apostolic times this seems to have been intimately connected with the Eucharist, and to have occasioned S. Paul's rebuke in 1 Cor. xi. 17 *foll.* by

---

[1] Ostendit non pane vivere hominem Dei sed Dei verbo.

[2] Matt. vii. 7.

[3] *de Bapt.* xx. *fin.* Igitur, Benedicti, quos gratia Dei expectat, cum de illo sanctissimo lavacro novi natalis ascenditis, et primas manus apud matrem cum fratribus aperitis, petite de Patre, petite de Domino peculia gratiae, distributiones charismatum subjacere. Petite et accipietis, inquit. Quaesistis enim, et invenistis : pulsastis, et aper-tum est vobis. Tantum oro, ut, cum petitis, etiam Tertulliani peccatoris memineritis.

reason of excesses in eating and drinking. By the
time of Pliny's letter to Trajan the two were separated, the Agape taking place in the evening, the
celebration of the Eucharist in early morning[1]. This
was also the case in North Africa in A.D. 200 as we see
from the passage in *de Corona* III., where Tertullian is
giving instances of customs of the Church due to
tradition and not to the direct command of Christ. "The
Sacrament of the Eucharist," he says, " was instituted
by our Lord at the time of food, and for general reception : but we receive it *also* at our gatherings before
daybreak, and only from the hand of the presiding
officers[2]."

We find in *Apolog.* XXXIX. *fin.* a more elaborate
account of the Agape. Here we read that there is
no ostentation or extravagance, no gluttony or drunken-
ness, but the surplus contributions are used for the
benefit of the poor. " Our supper from its very name
shews a reason for itself: it is called by the Greek
word for Love : however much it costs, it is gain to
incur the cost in the name of Religion, since we assist
all kinds of needy folk with comforts from it....In God's
sight, care for His poor is of greater value (than the
feasts of the heathen)[3]." The banquet begins with

---

[1] Plin. *Epist.* x. 96 ; cf. Lightfoot, *Ignatius*, I. 19 f.

[2] Eucharistiae sacramentum, et in tempore victus et omnibus man-
datum a Domino, etiam antelucanis coetibus nec de aliorum manu
quam praesidentium sumimus.

[3] Coena nostra de nomine rationem sui ostendit : Id vocatur quod

prayer, which is continued at intervals during the
night : eating, drinking, conversation are all conducted
as in the immediate presence of God[1]. Hands are then
washed[2], lights are brought in[3] and then Psalms and
Hymns are sung to God, either from the Holy Scriptures
or as each receives the word : and so general conversation ends the meeting, which breaks up so quietly and
in such orderly fashion that you would suppose the
guests had been not at a feast but at a religious
service[4].

Both in this passage (*Ap.* xxxix.) and also in *ad
Martyras* ii. mention is made of special doles sent from
the Agapai to Christians in prison.

Dilectio penes Graecos: quantiscumque sumptibus constet, lucrum
est pietatis nomine facere sumptum, si quidem inopes quosque
refrigerio isto juvamus...penes Deum major est contemplatio medio-
crium.

[1] Cf. the Quakers' Grace before meals "Lord Jesus, be thou our
guest."

[2] It must be remembered that the ancients, like people in the East
to-day, used no forks.

[3] Shewing that the Agape was held in late afternoon or evening.

[4] Non prius discumbitur quam oratio ad Deum praegustetur.
Editur quantum esurientes capiunt, bibitur quantum pudicis utile
est. Ita saturantur ut qui meminerint etiam per noctem adorandum
Deum sibi esse : ita fabulantur ut qui sciant Dominum audire. Post
aquam manualem et lumina, ut quisque de scripturis sanctis vel de
proprio ingenio potest, provocatur in medium Deo canere. Hinc pro-
batur quomodo biberit. Aeque oratio convivium dirimit. Inde dis-
ceditur non in catervas caesionium, nec in classes discursationum,
nec in eruptiones lasciviarum, sed ad eandem curam modestiae et
pudicitiae, ut qui non tam coenam caenaverint quam disciplinam.

"Let us compare the actual mode of life in the world and in prison, to see whether the spirit does not gain more in prison than the flesh loses. Nay, indeed, whatever is right, the flesh does not lose, owing to the care of the Church and the Love—the Agape—of the Brethren[1]."

Hence we may conclude that at Carthage in the days of Tertullian, the Agape of the Christians was closely connected with the distribution of charity. Monceaux indeed goes so far as to assert that the whole organization of Christianity resulted in its being " a vast mutual aid society[2]."

The same fact is apparent from the Acts of SS. Perpetua and Felicitas XVII.

On the other hand Tertullian the Montanist has much fault to find with the excesses for which these Love-Feasts offered opportunity. He even repeats the vile charges of the Heathen, such as we find detailed in Caecilius' speech in the *Octavius* of Minucius Felix (see below, p. 177, in ch. viii.), charges which Tertullian himself had repelled with much indignation in his

---

[1] *ad Mart.* II. Ipsam interim conversationem saeculi et carceris comparemus, si non plus in carcere spiritus acquirit, quam caro amittit. Immo et quae justa sunt caro non amittit per curam ecclesiae et agapen fratrum.—It is of course an open question whether the word Agape here refers to the Love-Feast or, generally, to the love of the Brethren.

[2] p. 21. La charité et la solidarité faisaient alors du Christianisme une vaste société de secours mutuels.

earlier days[1] (see *Apol.* VII., VIII., quoted below, §iv.,
pp. 72, 73). But in Cyprian's time, a generation later,
we find that the cause for such complaints had died out.

§ iv.   *The Eucharist.*

The central service of Christ's Religion is of course
frequently mentioned. Tertullian has varying names
for it: It is "an act of thanksgiving[2]," "the solemn
rites of the Lord[3]," the "supper of God[4]," the "banquet
of the Lord[5]," the "banquet of God[6]."

In *de Orat.* XIX. where he is discussing the question,
Is a Fast broken by receiving Holy Communion? he
calls the Eucharist the "Prayers of the sacrifices";
and he says, "With regard to regular Fast days (Wednesdays and Fridays), most think that there ought to
be no attendance at the Prayers of the sacrifices, on the
ground that the fast must cease with the reception of
the Lord's Body. Does the Eucharist then end an act
of obedience owed to God, or does it put you more

[1] Apud te agape in caccabis fervet, fides in culinis calet, spes in
ferculis jacet. Sed majoris est agape, quia per hunc adulescentes tui
cum sororibus dormiunt. Appendices scilicet gulae lascivia atque
luxuria est. *de Jejunio* XVII.

[2] *adv. Marc.* I. 23. Super panem...Deo gratiarum actionibus fungi-
tur.

[3] Dominica sollemnia celebramus. *de Fuga* XIV. ; so *de Anima* IX.
post transacta sollemnia.

[4] *de Spect.* XIII.   Caena Dei.

[5] Convivium Dominicum.   *ad Ux.* II., IV.

[6] Convivium Dei.   *ad Ux.* II., VIII.

in His debt? Will not your 'station'—your day of fasting—be all the more solemn if you have also stood at the altar of God? By the reception and reservation of the Lord's Body both points are secured, your sharing in the sacrifice and the observance of your duty (of fasting[1])."

The last extract gives us the familiar term "Eucharist," and speaks of it as "a sacrifice at the altar of God." It is to be noticed also that communicants were allowed to take the consecrated Bread home with them for private consumption at this period, a practice which was forbidden by councils at a later time. The same fact appears, *ad Uxorem* II., v., in the passage where Tertullian is urging the many difficulties besetting the Christian wife of a heathen husband. "How will you escape his notice when you get up during the night to pray? Will you not seem to him to be busy about some magic rites? Will your husband not know what it is you eat secretly before other food? If he knows that it is bread, does he not believe that it is what it is generally said to be?" (*viz.* bread soaked in infant's blood, or similar abominations[2]).

[1] De stationum diebus non putant plerique sacrificiorum orationibus interveniendum, quod statio solvenda sit accepto corpore Domini. Ergo devotum Deo obsequium eucharistia resolvit, an magis Deo obligat? Nonne sollemnior erit statio tua, si ad aram Dei steteris? accepto corpore Domini et reservato utrumque salvum est, et participatio sacrificii et executio officii.

[2] Latebisne tu cum...per noctem exurgis oratum, et non magiae aliquid videberis operari? non sciet maritus quid secreto ante omnem cibum gustes? et si sciverit panem, non illum credit esse qui dicitur?

The reception of the Eucharist before daybreak has been already alluded to[1]. The well-known passage from Pliny's letter to Trajan is quoted in the *Apology*, where we read that " with regard to the sacraments of the Christians he had found out nothing further than this—that they meet together before daybreak for the purpose of singing hymns to Christ and God," or, following another reading, " to Christ as God[2]."

The custom of celebrating the Eucharist in the early morning of the first day of the week was probably due to two causes: (1) That it might be a weekly memorial of the Lord's Resurrection (cf. Matt. xxviii. 1, ὀψὲ δὲ σαββάτων, τῇ ἐπιφωσκούσῃ εἰς μίαν σαββάτων: Mc. xvi. 2, λίαν πρωὶ τῇ μιᾷ τῶν σαββάτων...ἀνατείλαντος τοῦ ἡλίου. Lc. xxiv. 1, τῇ δὲ μιᾷ τῶν σαββάτων ὄρθρου βαθέως: Joh. xx. 1, τῇ δὲ μιᾷ τῶν σαββάτων ...πρωὶ σκοτίας ἔτι οὔσης) and (2) to avoid exciting undue attention and public notice. But the very secrecy of their service, to which only the initiated were admitted, roused suspicion, and very soon evil stories were circulated as to what took place. Eating the flesh of Christ and drinking His Blood, which the Christians said they met to do, lent itself to gross and malignant misinterpretation. They were accused of slaying infants, soaking bread in their blood, and eating the horrid food; after the Thyestean banquet followed

---

[1] See above, § iii. p. 67. *de Corona*, III. there quoted.

[2] Nihil aliud se de sacramentis eorum comperisse quam coetus antelucanos ad canendum Christo et (*v. l.* ut) Deo. *Apol.* II.

darkness, a dog being tied to the lamp and over-
turning it in his attempts to reach scraps offered to
him; and then came incest and nameless horrors[1].

Needless to say, Tertullian enters the most vehement protest against these unjustifiable and baseless
charges; nevertheless, at a later date he does not
scruple as a Montanist to hurl the same horrid accusations against the Catholics[2].

In his enumeration of heretical practices, Tertullian
implies that, in the orthodox Church, Catechumens are
not admitted to the sacred mysteries. In speaking of
the customs of heretics he says, "It is quite uncertain
who is a Catechumen (*i.e.* under instruction), who a
believer: they come together to the service, they listen
together as a congregation, they pray together, even
Gentiles if they happen to come in; they will toss
what is holy to the dogs, and pearls—though not real
pearls—before swine[3]."

---

[1] *Apol.* viii. "Infans tibi necessarius adhuc tener, qui nesciat
mortem, qui sub cultro tuo rideat: item panis, quo sanguinis virulen-
tiam colligas: praeterea candelabra et lucernae et canes aliqui et
offulae, quae illos ad eversionem luminum extendant: ante omnia
cum matre et sorore tua venire debebis." The same vile accusations
are enumerated in even greater detail in the *Octavius* of Min. Felix.
ix. See below, chap. viii. p. 177.

[2] See above, § iii. *sub fin.*

[3] *de Praescr. Haer.* xli. Quis catechumenus, quis fidelis, incertum
est : pariter adeunt, pariter audiunt, pariter orant, etiam Ethnici, si
superveniunt : sanctum canibus et porcis margaritas, licet non veras,
jactabunt.

But, for the earnest Christian, these services take
the place of games and other excitements which were
so attractive to the heathen. "The pleasures, the
spectacles, of Christians are holy, unceasing, without
charge. By them interpret your games of the circus,
in them see the courses run by the world, count the
lapse of time and space, look forward to the goal of the
end of all things, defend the gatherings of the churches,
rouse yourself at God's signal, awake at the angel's
trump, glory in the palms of martyrdom....Do you want
also blood ? you have Christ's[1]."

In his treatise on the Lord's Prayer, Tertullian, as
Cyprian does later[2], refers the fifth clause to the daily
Eucharist. "Give us to-day our daily bread" he says "has
a spiritual meaning: for Christ is our life, and bread is
our life (or *v. l.* the bread of life). I am, He says (Joh. vi.
35) the Bread of Life : and a little earlier (v. 33) the
Bread is the Word of the living God, which came down
from Heaven. Then because His Body also is reckoned

---

[1] Hae voluptates haec spectacula christianorum sancta, perpetua,
gratuita. In his tibi circenses ludos interpretare, cursus saeculi
intuere, tempora labentia, spatia, dinumera, metas consummationis
expecta, societates ecclesiarum defende, ad signum Dei suscitare, ad
tubam angeli erigere, ad Martyrii palmas gloriare....Vis autem et
sanguinis aliquid ? Habes Christi. *de Spectaculis,* xxix.

[2] *de Orat. Dominica,* xviii. Hunc autem panem dari nobis
quotidie postulamus, ne qui in Christo sumus, et eucharistiam quotidie
ad cibum salutis accipimus, intercedente aliquo graviore delicto, dum
abstenti et non communicantes a caelesti pane prohibemur, a Christi
corpore separemur.

as being in the Bread, This is my Body, He says. And so by asking for daily bread we pray that we may ever abide in Christ, never separated from his Body[1]."

In the same treatise (de Orat. III.) some have seen in Tertullian's reference to the angels' never ceasing song of Praise " Holy, Holy, Holy," an allusion to the " Ter Sanctus " in the Eucharistic service: but it perhaps refers only to Is. vi. 3 and Apoc. iv. 8[2].

That Bread and Wine are the elements essential to the Eucharist is clear from several passages : in adv. Marc. III. 19 Tertullian quotes a curious variant of both Ps. xcvi. 10 and Jerem. xi. 19 to press this point[3].

---

[1] de Oratione, vi. "Panem nostrum quotidianum da nobis hodie" spiritaliter potius intelligamus, Christus enim panis noster est, quia vita Christus et vita panis (v.l. vitae panis). Ego sum, inquit, panis vitae; et paullo supra, panis est sermo Dei vivi, qui descendit de caelis. (N.B. Vulg. Panis enim Dei est qui descendit, &c.) Tum quod et corpus ejus in pane censetur : Hoc est corpus meum. Itaque petendo panem quotidianum perpetuitatem postulamus in Christo et individuitatem a corpore ejus.

[2] Cui illa angelorum circumstantia non cessant dicere, Sanctus, Sanctus, Sanctus. Proinde igitur et nos angelorum, si meruerimus, candidati, jam hinc caelestem illam in Deum vocem et officium futurae claritatis ediscimus.

[3] The two passages run in LXX. thus : Ps. xcvi. (xcv.) 10, εἴπατε ἐν τοῖς ἔθνεσιν, ὁ κύριος ἐβασίλευσε, &c. : and Jer. xi. 19, δεῦτε καὶ ἐμβάλωμεν ξύλον εἰς τὸν ἄρτον αὐτοῦ, καὶ ἐκτρίψωμεν αὐτὸν, &c. and in Tertullian l.c. Dominus regnavit a ligno : and (here in agreement with the Vulgate), Venite, mittamus lignum in panem ejus, utique in corpus. Sic enim Deus in evangelio quoque vestro (sc. Marcionis and his party) revelavit, panem corpus suum appellans, ut et hinc jam eum intelligas corpori sui (? suo) figuram panis dedisse cujus retro corpus in panem prophetes figuravit, ipso Domino hoc sacramentum postea interpre-

Water is insufficient, as Cyprian says (*Epist.* LXIII. 1 *foll.*), unless mixed with wine : water is for baptism, not for sacrifice. As will be noticed below[1], a branch of the Montanists used cheese at the Eucharist, and were known as *Artoturitae*.

The elements themselves were treated with the utmost reverence, as is clear from *de Corona* III. "If any drop from the chalice or crumb of consecrated bread fall to the ground, it is a cause of great anxiety to us[2]."

Part of the ceremony at the Eucharistic service was the Kiss of Peace, the seal and sign of public prayer[3].

This pious observance some would omit, partly as savouring of ostentation, partly as being incompatible with days of fasting. Tertullian protests vigorously : "what prayer is complete," he asks, "if divorced from the Holy Kiss ? who when offering service to the Lord is

taturo.—The same passage occurs also *adv. Marc.* IV. 40, Adversus me cogitaverunt cogitatum, dicentes, Venite, conjiciamus lignum in panem ejus, scilicet crucem in corpus ejus (cf. also *adv. Jud.* x.).—And later, with reference to wine, Ut autem et sanguinis veterem figuram in vino recognoscas, aderit Esaias (lxiii. 1 *sq.*) &c.

[1] See below, ch. v. § ii. p. 136.

[2] Calicis aut panis etiam nostri aliquid decuti in terram anxie patimur.—An apt parallel is quoted by Oehler *ad loc.* from S. Augustine, ap. Gratian. I. 1. "Quanta sollicitudine observamus, quando nobis corpus Christi ministratur, ut nihil ex ipso de nostris manibus in terram cadat."

[3] Habita oratione cum fratribus...osculum pacis, quod est signaculum orationis. *de Oratione*, XVIII.

hindered by Peace? what sacrifice at the altar is there from which one retires without The Peace? whatever be the prayer, will it not be made more acceptable by our observing the command that we are 'not to appear unto men to fast'? (Matt. vi. 16). For we make it evident that we are fasting by our refusing the Kiss of Peace. You may abstain at home, where it is impossible to conceal the fact that you are fasting: but in public it is different: except on Good Friday when the fast is general and universal: then we act rightly in omitting the Kiss of Peace: for we have no reason to conceal what all are doing[1]."

The custom is also alluded to in the passage already quoted (*ad Uxor.* II. 4) where Tertullian asks, How will a pagan husband approve his wife exchanging kisses with other men[2]?

Litanies and public intercessions seem to have formed an important part of the Eucharistic service, which is called the "Crown of Prayer" in *de Orat.* XXVIII. while prayer is the spiritual sacrifice offered by God's

---

[1] *de Orat. l.c.* Quae oratio cum divortio sancti osculi integra? quem Domino officium facientem impedit pax? quale sacrificium est a quo sine pace receditur? quaecumque oratio (*v.l.* operatio) sit, non erit potior praecepti observatione quo jubemur jejunia nostra celare? Jam enim de abstinentia osculi agnoscimur jejunantes...sic et die Paschae, quo communis et quasi publica jejunii religio est, merito deponimus oscula, nihil curantes de occultando quod cum omnibus faciamus.

[2] Quis in carcerem ad osculanda vincula martyris reptare patietur? Jam vero alicui fratrum ad osculum convenire?

true priests to Him as a victim appropriate and acceptable[1].

The same fact may be inferred from the well-known passage about intercession for the Emperor in *Apol.* XXX. XXXI.

Tertullian's teaching about the sacrificial nature of the Holy Eucharist is clear. He speaks of the "altar" (*ara, altare*) which was no doubt the "*mensa*" or table marking the grave of some martyr or other departed saint, *e.g.* "Will not your 'statio,'—your day of fasting—be more solemn, if you also stand at God's altar[2]?" And in a passage in which he is calling attention to the teaching to be drawn from the two scape-goats (Lev. xvi. 5 f.), after reminding his readers that the one was mocked, cursed, spitted upon, torn, and wounded, and driven by the people to destruction outside of the camp, he goes on to say, "The other, offered as a sacrifice for sin, and handed over to be eaten by the Priests of the Temple only, gave marked proofs of the second type, whereby, after the expiation of all sins, the Priests of the spiritual Temple, *i.e.* of the Church, might enjoy, if I may say so, the very flesh of the grace of the Lord. Of this those who partake not are excluded from Salvation[3]."

[1] The passage is quoted in full above, see p. 19, n. 2.

[2] Nonne solemnior erit statio tua, si et ad aram Dei steteris? *de Orat.* XIX.

[3] Alter vero, pro delictis oblatus et sacerdotibus tantum templi in pabulum datus, secundae repraesentationis argumenta signabat, qua

From the passages already quoted we may infer the
order of the service of the Eucharist as celebrated at
Carthage in Tertullian's time. *Apol.* XXXIX.[1] describes
the gathering of the faithful in the early morning, the
prayers, the reading from Holy Scripture, the sermon,
the issuing of disciplinary or penitential notices, the
collection of Alms: from other passages we infer the
withdrawal at this point of Catechumens and non-
communicants: then follows the Kiss of Peace, the
consecration of the bread and wine by the bishop, or
a priest commissioned by him, in a chalice richly
decorated[2], and the distribution of the elements by the
deacons. The ceremony is concluded by prayers, and
the singing of psalms[3].

delictis omnibus expiatis sacerdotes templi spiritalis, id est ecclesiae,
Dominicae gratiae quasi visceratione quadam fruerentur, jejunantibus
ceteris a salute. *adv. Jud.* XIV.

[1] See above, § i. *in.*

[2] Tertullian speaks of chalices of the orthodox church ornamented
with the figure of the Good Shepherd: *de Pudic.* VII. Procedant ipsae
picturae calicum vestrorum, and again *ibid.* c. x. Pastor quem in
calice depingis.

[3] Reference may here be made to an exhaustive paper on
"Eucharistic Belief in the Second and Third Centuries" by Professor Swete, published in *Journ. Theol. Stud.* for Jan. 1902 (Vol. III.
p. 161 *foll.*).

§ v. *Prayer.*

a. The Treatise de Oratione.

There is good reason for thinking that Tertullian was ordained priest about the year 200 A.D. and that his three treatises on Baptism, Prayer, and Penitence, were written soon after that date, with a special view to the priestly instruction of his Catechumens. The first of the three has been already dealt with in § ii. of this chapter : the third will be found lower, § vi.

We may now briefly examine what he has to say about Prayer. "Prayer is the only means of conquering God," says Tertullian[1]; and its claims upon the Christian are constant and peremptory. " Prayer is the bulwark of our Faith, our arms of offence and defence against a foe who is watching us from all sides. Therefore let us never march without our arms[2]." He takes the Lord's Prayer as the basis of his Homily, discusses it clause by clause, and sees in it "not only the special characteristics of prayer, such as worship of God and petitions from man, but also almost the whole of the ' Word of the Lord,' and a complete reminder of discipline; so that really in the Lord's Prayer we find a compendium of the whole gospel[3]."

[1] *de Orat.* xxix. Sola est oratio quae Deum vincit.

[2] *ibid.* Oratio murus est Fidei, arma et tela nostra adversus hostem, qui nos undique observat. Itaque nunquam inermes incedamus.

[3] Neque enim propria tantum orationis officia complexa est, vel venerationem Dei aut hominis petitionem, sed omnem paene Sermo-

He summarizes its contents thus: "What an immense number of points are included within the short compass of these few words: utterances of prophets, evangelists, apostles; words of the Lord, parables, warnings, commands; what a number of duties are at once expressed! God's glory in 'the Father,' evidence of the Faith in 'the Name,' the sacrifice of obedience in 'the Will,' the assurance of hope in 'the Kingdom,' prayer for life in 'the Bread,' confession of debts in the petition for forgiveness, anxiety about temptations in the prayer for aid[1]."

He then goes on to discuss the true value of prayer, which is a spiritual exercise, and depends for its worth on the mind and right intention of the suppliant, rather than upon outward ritual acts; on his freedom from anger[2] rather than upon the cleanliness of his hands[3], or the stripping himself of his coat[4], or his sitting down for prayer[5], and so forth.

nem Domini, omnem commemorationem disciplinae, ut revera in oratione breviarium totius evangelii comprehendatur. *ibid.* I.

[1] Compendiis pauculorum verborum quot attinguntur edicta prophetarum, evangeliorum, apostolorum, sermones Domini, parabolae, exempla, praecepta! Quot simul expunguntur officia! Dei Honor in Patre, Fidei testimonium in Nomine, oblatio obsequii in Voluntate, commemoratio spei in Regno, petitio vitae in Pane, exomologesis debitorum in Deprecatione, sollicitudo temptationum in Postulatione Tutelae. *ibid.* IX.

[2] *ibid.* XI.

[3] *ibid.* XIII.

[4] Est quorundam expositis paenulis orationem facere. *ibid.* XVI.

[5] *ibid.* XVI.

Incidentally, he gives us much information as to observances of the orthodox Church in prayer, some of which are noticed below. Besides regular morning and evening prayer, which he takes for granted[1], he would have the third, sixth, and ninth hours every day sanctified by prayer; also that grace before meat should not be omitted, nor prayer forgotten before going to the daily bath[2].

He concludes his treatise with what to some may seem a fanciful utterance, but surely it is a burst of genuine eloquence. "Even angels pray, all of them; all creatures pray: cattle and wild beasts pray and bend their knees; when they come forth from their stalls, or caves, they look up to heaven with eager eyes, snorting and breathing deep as their custom is. Nay, even the birds as they rise from their nest, soar skyward, and open their wings as men their hands, in the shape of a cross, and utter something which surely seems like Prayer. What more can I say about the duty of Prayer? just this: The Lord Himself prayed, to whom be assigned Honour and Worth for ever and ever[3]."

[1] Legitimis orationibus, quae sine ulla admonitione debentur ingressu lucis et noctis. *ibid.* xxv.

[2] Cibum non prius sumere, et lavacrum non prius adire quam interposita oratione fideles decet. *ibid.* xxv.

[3] Orant etiam angeli omnes; orat omnis creatura; orant pecudes et ferae et genua declinant, et egredientes de stabulis ac speluncis ad caelum non otioso ore suspiciunt, vibrantes spiritum suo more. Sed

b. Turning to the East in prayer.

In the parallel passages *Apol.* XVI. and *ad Nationes* I. 13, we find that in N. Africa as elsewhere in Christendom[1] it was generally customary to turn to the East in prayer, as the source of light, and symbolic of Christ the Sun of Righteousness. This custom led to a charge against the Christians of worshipping the sun, a charge confirmed by the fact that the first day of the week, the day of the sun, was especially devoted by the Church to joy and gladness[2]. Tertullian treats this charge with the same scorn he pours on the accusation that the Christians' God is an ass or an ass's head (*Ap. l.c.*).

c. Attitude in Prayer.

To pray kneeling was associated with humiliation, penance, and fasting: and so we find that during the joyous season between Easter and Whitsuntide, not only were the regular fasts—on Wednesdays and Fridays —not observed, but also prayers were said standing.

et aves nido exurgentes eriguntur ad caelum, et alarum crucem pro manibus expandunt, et dicunt aliquid quod oratio videatur. Quid ergo amplius de officio orationis? Etiam ipse Dominus oravit, cui sit honor et virtus in secula seculorum. *ibid.* XXIX. *fin.*

[1] Cf. *Apost. Constitutions*, II. 57; Aug. *de Serm. Dom.* II. 5; Bingham, *Eccl. Ant.* XIII. 8, 15.

[2] *ad Nat. l.c.* alii...solem Christianum Deum aestimant, quod innotuerit ad orientis partem facere nos precationem, vel die solis laetitiam curare.

The same difference in the attitude of those praying was also made on Sundays, and Tertullian speaks of "some few" who abstained from kneeling on Saturdays also, the Jewish Sabbath. "As to kneeling in Prayer different customs are permissible. There are some few who do not kneel on the Sabbath (Saturday)....We, however, as we have been taught, on the day of the Lord's Resurrection only, ought to be free not merely from the humiliation of kneeling, but also from all that entails anxiety and all serious duties, putting off even our business, for fear we should give place to the Devil. The same also applies to the interval between Easter and Whitsuntide, which we mark with the like solemn exultation[1]." So, "on the Lord's Day we consider it wrong to fast, or to pray on our knees. We enjoy this same liberty from the day of the Passover right on to Pentecost[2]." On the other hand, kneeling is customary at other times, at early morning prayers, on fast days, and "station days[3]," &c.

---

[1] De genu quoque ponendo varietatem observationis patitur oratio per pauculos quosdam qui Sabbato abstinent genibus...nos vero, sicut accepimus, solo die Dominicae Resurrectionis non ab isto tantum, sed omni anxietatis habitu et officio cavere debemus, differentes etiam negotia, ne quem diabolo locum demus. Tantundem et spatio Pentecostes, quod eadem exultationis solemnitate dispungimus. *de Orat.* XXIII.

[2] Die Dominico jejunium nefas ducimus, vel de geniculis adorare. Eadem immunitate a die Paschae in Pentecosten usque gaudemus. *de Cor.* III. *Cf.* below p. 94 n.

[3] Ceterum omni die quis dubitet prosternere se Deo vel prima

Tertullian often alludes to the outstretched arms and opened hands of the suppliant, which, as he reminds us, take the form of a cross, *e.g.* " We not only raise our hands (in prayer) but also open them wide, both when we celebrate the Lord's Passion and when in prayer we make confession to Christ[1]." Again, " If you set up a man with outstretched hands, you at once make the shape of a cross[2]." So, " We Christians pray, looking up to heaven, with hands expanded because they are free from guilt, with head bared, because we have no cause for shame[3]." Horace's Caelo supinas si tuleris manus nascente luna, rustica Phidyle, &c. (*Car.* iii. 23. 1) will of course occur to everybody.

But Tertullian is careful to add that these out-stretched hands must be raised modestly and humbly, not too high nor with arrogance : nor must the face be too bold. We must take warning from the diverse attitudes of the Pharisee and the Publican, if we wish

saltem oratione qua lucem ingredimur? Jejuniis autem et stationibus nulla oratio sine genu et reliquo humilitatis more celebranda est. *de Orat.* XXIII.

[1] Nos vero non attollimus tantum, sed etiam expandimus, et de Dominica Passione modulati et orantes confitemur Christo. *de Orat.* XIV.

[2] Si statueris hominem manibus expansis, imaginem crucis feceris. *ad Nat.* I. 12.

[3] Illuc suspicientes Christiani manibus expansis, quia innocuis, capite nudo, quia non erubescimus...oramus. *Apol.* XXX. Oehler *ad loc.* quotes Prudentius in Martyrio Fructuosi (*Peristeph.* VI. 103 *seq.*). Palmas in morem crucis ad Patrem levandas.

to adopt that which will be the more well pleasing to God[1].

d. Prayers for the Dead.

This custom so natural to the instincts of the human heart was universally recognized in the Church of North Africa. Not to mention the touching passages in the Acts of S. Perpetua and S. Felicitas[2]—Perpetua's confident prayer from prison for her dead brother, and her comfort in its answer—we find such expressions as these in Tertullian's writings:—

"The wife intercedes for the soul of her (dead husband), and prays for refreshment for him in the meantime, and in the first resurrection to be reunited to him: on the anniversaries of his death she offers the Eucharist that he may enjoy rest[3]."

In arguing against second marriages he says, "Nor indeed will you be able to hate your former wife, for whom you preserve an even more scrupulous affection

[1] Atqui cum modestia et humilitate adorantes magis commenda-mus Deo preces nostras, ne ipsis quidem manibus sublimius elatis, sed temperate ac probe elatis, ne vultu quidem in audaciam erecto. Nam ille publicanus, qui non tantum prece, sed et vultu humiliatus atque dejectus orabat, justificatior Pharisaeo procacissimo discessit. de Orat. XVII.

[2] See Acta vii. dealt with elsewhere: see pp. 131, 135.

[3] de Monogamia, x. Pro anima eius (sc. defuncti mariti) orat, et refrigerium interim adpostulat ei, et in prima resurrectione con-sortium, et offert annuis diebus dormitionis ejus.

(than you had for her while living), as for one already received into the presence of the Lord; for whose spirit you offer intercession, for whom you render yearly oblations[1]." Again, in his list of customs sanctioned by tradition not directly ordered in Holy Scripture, he says, " We make oblations for the Dead, for their birth into life every year on the day of their death[2]."

Professor Swete in an exhaustive article on the subject of Prayer for the Dead in the first four centuries[3] calls attention to the fact that the " Church in North Africa was the first community, so far as we know, which offered the Eucharist for the benefit of the departed." This may have been due in the first instance to Montanistic influences, but it soon became general at Carthage: and in the next generation there is constant allusion to the practice in the writings of Cyprian[4].

---

[1] de Exhortatione Castitatis, XI. Neque enim pristinam poteris odisse, cui etiam religiosiorem reservas affectionem, ut jam receptae apud Dominum, pro cujus spiritu postulas, pro qua oblationes annuas reddis.

[2] de Corona, III. Oblationes pro defunctis, pro nataliciis annua die facimus.

[3] Journ. Theol. Stud. Vol. VIII. No. 32 for July 1907 ; cf. also Vol. III. p. 167.

[4] See Monceaux, p. 59.

§ vi. *Penance and the Forgiveness of Sins.*

The whole question of Penitential Discipline in the first three centuries has been very fully treated by Professor Swete in the *Journal of Theological Studies*, April 1903, and he has left but little to say on this subject so far as the Church in North Africa is concerned. Tertullian's authorship of the treatise *de Paenitentia* has been questioned, but without sufficient grounds. In it he recognizes that by Baptism plenary remission of sins is secured[1]. "Baptism is the sign and seal of our Faith in Jesus Christ, that we are living in the Spirit and not according to the flesh: that being so, we are baptized not in order that we may sin no more, but because we have ceased to sin, for we are already cleansed in heart."

On the other hand if a Christian after Baptism does commit sin, what can be done ? Tertullian replies that a door of repentance is open to him once and only once after public confession duly made (*Exomologesis*). The degradation of this public humiliation must be faced or there can be no reconciliation, no forgiveness. It is the only hope of salvation as is the plank to the shipwrecked sailor[2].

---

[1] *de Paen.* VI. Lavacrum illud obsignatio est fidei, quae fides a paenitentiae fide incipitur et commendatur. Non ideo abluimur ut delinquere desinamus, sed quia desiimus, quoniam jam corde loti sumus.

[2] *ibid.* VII. Deus clausa jam ignoscentiae janua et instinctionis sera obstructa aliquid adhuc permisit patere. Collocavit in vestibulo

Tertullian gives a full definition and description of *Exomologesis*—Public Confession—in the following words: " As to dress and food, the Penitent is bidden to lie in sack-cloth and ashes, to cover his body with filth, to prostrate his mind with grief, to make full and sorrowful compensation for his wrongdoing; he must be content for the future with the plainest food and drink[1], not of course on account of appetite but for the sake of his soul; he must assist his prayers by frequent fasts, groan, weep, and howl day and night to the Lord his God, fling himself down before the Presbyters, embrace the knees of those Beloved of God (the Martyrs and Confessors), and entreat all the Brethren to use their intercessions on his behalf. Such is the rite of *Exomologesis* the object of which is to ensure penance, and from fear of future danger to honour the Lord now: by itself pronouncing against the sinner, it takes the place of God's indignation, and by temporary affliction it anticipates—I will not say frustrates—the punishment of Eternity[2]."

paenitentiam secundam, quae pulsantibus patefaciat, sed jam semel, quia, jam secundo: sed amplius nunquam, quia proxime frustra. *ibid.* IX. Exomologesis...qua delictum Domino nostrum confitemur... quatenus satisfactio confessione disponitur...prosternendi et humilificandi hominis disciplina est. *ibid.* IV. Paenitentia vita est...eam tu peccator ita amplexare ut naufragus alicujus tabulae fidem.

[1] *i.e.* bread and water: cf. *de Patien.* XIII. where he is also describing the course of *Exomologesis*, Sordes cum angustia victus Domino libat, contenta simplici pabulo puroque aquae potu.

[2] De ipso quoque habitu atque victu mandat sacco et cineri incubare, corpus sordibus obscurare, animum maeroribus dejicere, illa

Strict as this discipline was, Tertullian adopts an even severer line as Montanist. In his treatise *de Pudicitia*, which is a violent protest against the action of Pope Callistus in issuing an edict "I remit, after penance done, the sins of adultery and fornication[1]," Tertullian upholds Montanistic severity as against the leniency towards penitents favoured by the party then in power at Rome. In particular he finds fault with the *Shepherd* of Hermas[2], who in Tertullian's opinion had not been sufficiently severe towards penitents after sins of impurity[3].

He protests also against Callistus' claim to have the right of remitting sins by his office of Bishop, in the case of all sins, after Baptism, though he concedes this right in the case of more venial offences[4].

quae peccavit tristi tractatione mutare, ceterum pastum et potum pura nosse, non ventris scilicet sed animae causa, plerumque vero jejuniis preces alere, ingemiscere, lacrimari, et mugire dies noctesque ad Dominum Deum tuum, Presbyteris advolvi et caris Dei adgeniculari, omnibus fratribus legationes deprecationis suae injungere. Haec omnia exomologesis, ut paenitentiam commendet, ut de periculi timore Dominum honoret, ut in peccatorem ipsa pronuntians pro Dei indignatione fungatur, et temporali afflictatione aeterna supplicia, non dicam frustretur, sed expungat. *de Paen.* IX.

[1] Ego et moechiae et fornicationis delicta paenitentia functis dimitto. *de Pud.* I.

[2] *ibid.* X. Scriptura Pastoris quae sola moechos amat; and again XX. Receptior apud ecclesias epistola Barnabae illo apocrypho Pastore moechorum.

[3] Professor Bigg in his *Origins of Christianity*, p. 73, shares to the full Tertullian's disapproval of this writer.

[4] Salva illa paenitentiae specie post fidem, quae aut levioribus delictis veniam ab episcopo consequi poterit, aut majoribus et inremissibilibus a Deo solo. *de Pudic.* XVIII. *fin.*

There is a marked change of view between Tertullian the orthodox priest and Tertullian the Montanist. He wrote the *de Paenitentia* while still catholic, and considered then that all sins after Baptism could find forgiveness at least once (as shewn above): in *adv. Marc.* IV. 9, he enumerates the seven deadly sins "Idolatry, Blasphemy, Murder, Adultery, Fornication, False Witness, Fraud[1]," the list being evidently based on S. Matt. xv. 19, "For out of the heart proceed evil thoughts, murders, adulteries, fornications, thefts, false witness, blasphemies[2]." He gives no hint that any of these were outside the possibility of pardon by the Church. But by the time he wrote the *de Pudicitia*, he had learnt—mindful no doubt of the distinction drawn in 1 John v. 16, between "sins unto death" and "sins not unto death"— to place certain sins outside of the pale of forgiveness altogether. Some, he says, will be remissible, others not: just as no one doubts that some deserve scourging, others damnation[3]. In the latter class are mainly three, idolatry, uncleanness, murder. But these extreme views did not commend themselves to the orthodox Church at large, and by degrees the weakness

[1] Septem maculis capitalium delictorum...idolatria, blasphemia, homicidio, adulterio, stupro, falso testimonio, fraude.

[2] *Cf.* 1 Cor. v. 11.

[3] *de Pud.* II. Alia erunt remissibilia, alia irremissibilia: secundum quod nemini dubium est alia castigationem mereri, alia damnationem.

of human nature enforced the recognition of a laxer discipline.

It is clear then that the ritual of *Exomologesis* or Public Confession was rigidly exacted before a Penitent could be reconciled, after sin, to the conscience of the community. But it is worth noticing that all this penance was undergone publicly : there is no trace in North Africa, in Tertullian's days, of the practice of Auricular Confession and private Absolution.

§ vii. *Liturgy.*

We have practically no trace left of the form of service used in the North African Church, but the references to it are frequent, especially in the writings of Tertullian. It is very important as being the most ancient Latin Liturgy, for even in A.D. 200 the Church in Rome was still speaking Greek, and its public services and literature belonged to that language and not to Latin.

At first of course neither at Carthage nor at Rome nor elsewhere was there any " Christian year" properly so called: the Ecclesiastical Calendar was built up round the weekly memorial of Christ's Resurrection, the Eucharist celebrated at dawn on the first day of each week : prominence was naturally assigned to the Festival of Festivals, Easter Day, and the recognition of that great Feast, aided by the Festivals of Martyrs—

i.e. the annual celebrations of their death—by degrees reached the full observance of the Christian year.

By Tertullian's time the observance of the Jewish Sabbath by Christians had been completely abandoned in North Africa and probably elsewhere[1]. Not that the Sabbath was not a Divine institution, but that it had served its time, and its place was now taken by the Christian Sunday, the Lord's Day[2], as Tertullian calls it *l.c.* and again a little later, " The Gentiles have their festival day once a year in each case, for you it comes once a week[3]."

He discusses the whole question of Sabbath observance in *adv. Marc.* IV. 12, where he argues from the episode of the healing of the withered hand on the Sabbath (Lc. vi. 1—11) that Christ as Lord of the Sabbath came not to destroy but to fulfil: he enlightened the Mosaic law of Sabbath observance by a higher law, that it is lawful to do good on the sabbath days, a principle which was recognized even in Mosaic times by carrying the ark of the Covenant round the walls of Jericho for seven days, including at least one Sabbath day[4], and so the way is prepared for the trans-

---

[1] *de Idol.* XIV. Nobis quibus sabbata extranea sunt.

[2] Dominicus dies.

[3] Ethnicis semel annuus dies quisque festus est, tibi octavo quoque die. *de Idol.* XIV.

[4] Per Jesum (*i.e.* Joshua) tunc quoque concussum est Sabbatum, ut et hoc in Christum renuntiaretur. Cf. *adv. Jud.* IV.

It is curious that this passage seems to be quoted as referring to Christ and not to Joshua by both Leclercq (*Afrique Chrétienne* I. p. 66) and Cabrol (*Dict. d'Archéologie chrétienne, s.v.* Africa).

ference of the observance of the seventh to the first day in each week. The letter passes, but the spirit lives: and one seventh of our time remains dedicated to God.

The "Lord's Day" was festal: on it fasting was forbidden and also to pray on bended knee: the same custom applied to all the fifty days between Easter and Pentecost[1].

The week clusters round the Sunday; and Wednesdays and Fridays are *Dies Stationum, i.e.* days of special fasting and prayer[2]. The metaphor *statio* comes from the military term for what we should call "sentry duty[3]," but while the fast was not prolonged by the Church beyond the ninth hour (cf. *Didache*), the Montanists had no such limit[4]. The special hours of

---

[1] *de Corona,* III. and *de Orat.* XXIII. both quoted above § ii. p. 84. *Cf.* also *ibid.* XI. Jam et stationes (*i.e.* fixed hours for prayer and fasting) aut aliis magis faciet (sc. miles) quam Christo, aut et Dominico die, quando nec Christo? Oehler quotes several passages illustrative of this custom (*de Cor.* III.) notably a fragment of Irenaeus, ἐν τῇ κυριακῇ μὴ κλίνειν γόνυ σύμβολόν ἐστι τῆς ἀναστάσεως, δι' ἧς τῇ τοῦ Χριστοῦ χάριτι τῶν τε ἁμαρτημάτων καὶ τοῦ ἐπ' αὐτῶν τεθανατωμένου θανάτου ἠλευθερώθημεν. "Not to kneel on the Lord's Day is a symbol of the Resurrection, by means of which through the grace of Christ we were set free both from our sins and from the death incurred by them."

[2] Stationum quae et ipsae suos quidem dies habeant quartae feriae et sextae. *de Jejunio,* II. Cf. *Pastor Hermae Simil.* 5 (Kolberg, p. 172).

[3] *de Orat.* XIX. Statio de militari exemplo nomen accepit, nam et militia Dei sumus. See Lewis and Short, *s.v.*

[4] *de Jejunio* X. Atque stationes nostras ut indictas, quidam vero et in serum constitutas, novitatis nomine incusant, hoc quoque munus

prayer remained as in former times, the third, the sixth, and the ninth[1]: but Tertullian disclaims special directions as to hours of prayer[2].

We find the elementary ritual of the marriage service summarized at the end of *ad Uxorem* II. where we read, " How can we sufficiently describe the joy of that marriage, which is approved of by the Church, confirmed by the Eucharist, sealed by solemn ' Bene-diction,' witnessed by Angels, ratified by the Father[3]? "

Incidentally it may be noticed that Tertullian is careful to mention, "Divorce is forbidden except for the cause of fornication[4]." (Cf. S. Matt. v. 32 : xix. 9.)

To recapitulate, we trace the rudiments of liturgical organization in the observance of Easter, Pentecost, Sunday, Days of Station during the week, and the anniversaries of the Death of Martyrs: but we find in Tertullian's writings no allusion to any observance of the Festivals of Christmas Day, the Epiphany, or Ascension Day, or of the season of Lent : none of

et ex arbitro obeundum esse dicentes et non ultra nonam detinendum de suo scilicet more.

[1] *de Jejunio* III. X. XIII.

[2] *de Orat.* XXIII. De temporibus orationis nihil omnino praescrip-tum est nisi plane omni in tempore et loco orare : with reference to 1 Tim. ii. 8. Βούλομαι οὖν προσεύχεσθαι τοὺς ἄνδρας ἐν παντὶ τόπῳ ἐπαίροντας ὁσίους χεῖρας χωρὶς ὀργῆς καὶ διαλογισμοῦ.

[3] Unde sufficiamus ad enarrandam felicitatem ejus matrimonii quod ecclesia conciliat, et confirmat oblatio, et obsignat benedictio, angeli renuntiant, Pater rato habet? *ad Ux.* II. viii.

[4] Denique (spiritus) divortium prohibet, nisi stupri causa. *ad Ux.* II. ii.

which seem to have been generally recognized before
the middle of the fourth century[1]. The order of
service observed by the Brethren at their regular
meetings has been preserved for us by Tertullian in
Apol. XXXIX., and has been already quoted[2]. It was
evidently of a more or less informal character, though
the outlines were stereotyped and constant, and con-
sisted of Bible reading, prayer, preaching, the enforce-
ment of discipline, almsgiving. For the order of
service at Baptism and the Eucharist, see the sections
of this chapter under those heads.

§ viii.   *The Creed.*

That the Apostles' Creed—practically in its present
shape—was in use for the instruction of Catechumens
in the Church of North Africa A.D. 200 is clear from
three cardinal passages of Tertullian, each of which it
may be advisable to quote in full. The most concise
form we find in *de Virg. Velandis* I. " Our Rule of
Faith is altogether One, standing alone, not to be shaken,
unchangeable, the Rule, that is, of believing in One
only God, the Omnipotent, the Creator of the Universe,
and in His Son Jesus Christ, born of the Virgin Mary,
crucified under Pontius Pilate, raised again the third
day from the dead, received in the Heavens, sitting
now at the right hand of the Father, about to come

[1] See Monceaux, pp. 24, 25.   [2] See above, § i. p. 42.

to judge the quick and the dead through the Resurrection also of the flesh." He goes on to speak of the sending of the Paraclete, the Holy Spirit[1].

At somewhat greater length in *adv. Prax.* II. " We however (*i.e.* in contrast with heretics who speak of the Incarnation and Passion of the Father) from the earliest times and still more now when we have better instruction through the Paraclete, the Guide into all Truth, we believe that God indeed is One, but under this dispensation which we call in Greek *Oeconomy* (*i.e.* management or government), in such fashion that there is also a Son of the one God, His Word, Who proceeded from Himself, by Whom all things were made, and without Whom was made nothing. (We believe) that He was sent by the Father into a Virgin and born of Her, Man and God, Son of Man and Son of God, and named Jesus Christ: that this (Jesus Christ) suffered, that He died and was buried, according to the Scriptures, and was raised by the Father, and being received up again in Heaven sitteth at the right hand of

[1] Regula quidem fidei una omnino est, sola immobilis et irreformabilis, credendi scilicet in unicum Deum omnipotentem, mundi conditorem, et Filium Ejus Jesum Christum, natum ex Virgine Maria, crucifixum sub Pontio Pilato, tertia die resuscitatum a mortuis, receptum in caelis, sedentem nunc ad dexteram Patris, venturum judicare vivos et mortuos per carnis etiam Resurrectionem...cum propterea Paracletum miserit Dominus, ut quoniam humana mediocritas omnia semel capere non poterat, paulatim dirigeretur et ordinaretur et ad perfectum perduceretur disciplina ab illo Vicario Domini, Spiritu Sancto.

D. 7

the Father, and shall come to judge the quick and the
dead: furthermore He sent from His Father, according
to His own promise, the Holy Spirit, the Paraclete,
Who sanctifieth the faith of those who believe in the
Father and the Son and the Holy Spirit[1]."

The third passage is perhaps the most complete:
de Praescr. Haeret. XIII. " Our Rule of Faith—in order
that we may now declare what it is we maintain—is
that whereby belief is professed that God is wholly one,
and none other than the Creator of the World, who
produced all things out of nothing through His Word
sent down first of all: that Word, called His Son, seen
in divers manners in the name of God by the Patriarchs,
ever heard of in the Prophets, at last was brought
down by the Spirit and Power of God the Father into
the Virgin Mary, was made flesh in her womb, and
being born of her went forth[2] as Jesus Christ: after
that He preached the New Law and the New Promise

---

[1] Nos vero et semper et nunc magis, ut instructiores per Paracletum, Deductorem scilicet omnis veritatis, unicum quidem Deum
credimus, sub hac tamen dispensatione quam οἰκονομίαν dicimus, ut
unici Dei sit et Filius Sermo Ipsius, qui ex Ipso processerit, per quem
omnia facta sunt et sine quo factum est nihil. Hunc missum a Patre
in Virginem et ex ea natum, Hominem et Deum, Filium hominis et
Filium Dei, et cognominatum Jesum Christum : Hunc passum, Hunc
mortuum et sepultum, secundum scripturas, et resuscitatum a Patre,
et in caelo resumptum sedere ad dexteram Patris, venturum judicare
vivos et mortuos : Qui exinde miserit, secundum promissionem suam,
a Patre Spiritum Sanctum Paracletum, Sanctificatorem fidei eorum
qui credunt in Patrem et Filium et Spiritum Sanctum.

[2] The text here is uncertain.

of the Kingdom of Heaven, wrought mighty works, was crucified, and on the third day rose again, was caught up into heaven, and sat on the right hand of the Father: He sent instead of Himself the Power of the Holy Spirit to lead the Faithful; He shall come with glory to receive His Saints into the enjoyment of eternal life and celestial promises, and to judge the wicked by never ending fire, the resurrection of both just and unjust being accompanied by the restoration of the flesh[1]."

The first two of these passages were certainly written after Tertullian had become a Montanist: but all three represent accurately enough the belief of the orthodox Church at the time. It is worth while calling attention to the fact that the clause "He descended into Hell" is absent from all three versions of the Creed, while in the second only is any

[1] Regula est autem fidei, ut jam hinc quid defendamus profiteamur, illa scilicet qua creditur unum omnino Deum esse nec alium praeter mundi Conditorem, Qui universa de nihilo produxerit per Verbum suum primo omnium demissum: Id Verbum Filium ejus appellatum, in nomine Dei varie visum a patriarchis, in Prophetis semper auditum, postremo delatum ex Spiritu Patris Dei et virtute in Virginem Mariam, carnem factum in utero ejus et ex ea natum exisse Jesum Christum, exinde praedicasse novam legem et novam promissionem regni caelorum, virtutes fecisse, crucifixum tertia die resurrexisse, in caelos ereptum sedisse ad dexteram Patris, misisse vicariam vim Spiritus Sancti, qui credentes agat, venturum cum claritate ad sumendos sanctos in vitae aeternae et promissorum caelestium fructum et ad profanos judicandos igni perpetuo, facta utriusque partis resuscitatione cum carnis restitutione.

precise statement made of Christ's death and burial. The later clauses of the Apostles' Creed, as it has come down to us, had not yet been formulated.

To these three passages may be added a fourth, interesting as shewing the influence of Rome on African Christianity, and embodying the embryo creed common to both Carthage and Rome. "Let us see," he says, "what she—*sc.* the Church of Rome—has learnt, taught, and communicated also to the African Churches. She acknowledges that there is One God, the Lord, the Creator of the World, and Christ Jesus, born of the Virgin Mary, Son of God the Creator; and she acknowledges the Resurrection of the Flesh: she unites the Law and the Prophets with the writings of the Evangelists and the Apostles: thence she derives her Faith: this Faith she seals with water, clothes with the Holy Spirit, feeds with the Eucharist, exhorts to undergo martyrdom; and so it is that she admits no candidate, except in agreement with this formulary[1]."

---

[1] *de Praescr. Haeret.* xxxvi. Videamus quid didicerit, quid docuerit, cum Africanis quoque ecclesiis contesseravit. Unum Deum Dominum novit, Creatorem universitatis, et Christum Jesum ex Virgine Maria Filium Dei Creatoris, et carnis resurrectionem; Legem et Prophetas cum Evangelicis et Apostolicis literis miscet; inde potat Fidem; eam aqua signat, Sancto Spiritu vestit, Eucharistia pascit, martyrium exhortatur, et ita adversus hanc Institutionem neminem recipit.

§ ix.   *The Cross.*

From the days of S. Paul the Cross became the symbol of Christianity[1], anticipated even by our Lord's own words, "If any man will come after Me, let him take up his Cross," &c.[2]   Hence we find the Cross,—the symbol of Christ's Passion and Death to the Christian, as it was the embodiment of everything that was criminal and degrading for the Heathen—treated with the utmost reverence in the Church of North Africa: so much so that Tertullian finds it necessary in a passage of sustained irony (*Apolog.* XVI.) to defend his co-religionists from the absurd charge of worshipping the Cross.   " The man who thinks that we are full of reverence for the Cross, will himself be our fellow-worshipper.   When a piece of wood is worshipped, it makes no difference what is the fashion of it, so long as the quality of the material is the same ; it makes no difference what is its shape, provided that it be the very body of the God.   And yet in what way is Pallas of Athens distinguished from the stump of a cross, and Ceres of Pharos (*i.e.* Isis), who without any effigy are set up as consisting of a rude stake and shapeless log ? Any piece of wood fixed in an upright position is part

---

[1] "God forbid that I should glory save in the Cross," &c. ; cf. 1 Cor. i. 18, 23, &c.

[2] S. Luke ix. 23, &c.

of a cross.   We—if we *do* worship the Cross—at least worship it as a God whole and entire[1]."

The same line of argument in almost the same words is used in the parallel passage *ad Nationes* I. xii. "The man who declares we are Priests of the Cross, will himself be our fellow-worshipper: the quality of a cross—what constitutes a cross—is that it should be the symbol made of wood: you also in your rites worship the (symbol) made of that material in the shape of an effigy.   Though just as your (symbol) is a human figure, so also ours is of its own proper shape. Never mind about the outline, provided there be one and the same quality: never mind about the shape, provided it be the very Body of the God.   But if proceeding from this a difference intervenes, how is Pallas of Athens distinguished from the stump of a cross, and Ceres of Pharos (*sc.* Isis) who without shape is represented as consisting of a rude stake and a single upright beam of shapeless log?   Any piece of wood fixed in an upright position is part of a cross and indeed its chief part.   But to us the whole Cross is assigned (as an object of worship) that is to say with its transverse

---

[1] Sed et qui crucis nos religiosos putat, consecraneus erit noster, cum lignum aliquod propitiatur.   Viderit habitus, cum materiae qualitas eadem sit: viderit forma, dum id ipsum corpus Dei sit.   Et tamen quanto distinguitur a crucis stipite Pallas Attica et Ceres Pharia, quae sine effigie rudi palo et informi ligno prostat?   Pars crucis est omne robur quod erecta statione defigitur.   Nos, si forte, integrum et totum Deum colimus.

beam and its excrescence serving as seat. In this respect then you are the more blameworthy, who have dedicated a mutilated and uncompleted log, which others (as you say) have consecrated fully formed and complete[1]."

In the *Octavius* of Minucius Felix, the charge is dealt with in more direct fashion (XXIX.): "We neither worship the Cross, nor have we any wish to do so[2]." The author proceeds to bring against the heathen the same countercharge as we find in Tertullian, *viz.* that the Romans in the excessive reverence paid to their standards, trophies, &c., are guilty of just that idolatry which they ascribe falsely to the Christians, when they accuse them of worshipping the Cross.

That great reverence was paid to the Sign of the Cross, and that it was constantly in use, is clear from several passages: *e.g. de Corona* III. "Whenever we start on a journey, in all our goings out and comings in,

---

[1] Sed et qui nos crucis antistites affirmat, consecraneus erit noster. Crucis qualitas signum est de ligno : etiam de materia colitis penes vos cum effigie. Quanquam sicut vestrum humana figura est, ita et nostrum sua propria. Viderint nunc lineamenta dum una sit qualitas: viderit forma, dum ipsum sit Dei Corpus. Quod si de hoc differentia intercedit, quanto distinguitur a crucis stipite Pallas Attica et Ceres Pharia quae sine forma rudi palo et solo staticulo ligni informis repraesentatur? Pars crucis et quidem majus est omne robur quod derecta statione defigitur. Sed nobis tota crux imputatur, cum antemna scilicet sua et cum illo sedilis excessu. Hoc quidem vos incusabiliores qui mutilum et truncum dicastis lignum, quod alii plenum et structum consecraverunt.

[2] Cruces etiam nec colimus nec optamus.

when we put on our clothes or our shoes, when we enter the bath, when we begin our dinner, when the lights are brought in, when we go to bed or sit down to rest, in whatever way our daily life calls upon us, we mark our forehead with the sign of the Cross[1]." So *ad Uxorem* II. 5: in a passage already referred to: "Can you hope to escape the notice of your heathen husband when you make the sign of the Cross on your bed or on your own person[2]?" The same custom is implied in *adv. Marc.* III. 22, where in quoting Ezek. ix. 4 "The Lord said unto him, Go through the midst of the city, through the midst of Jerusalem, and set a mark upon the foreheads of the men that sigh and that cry for all the abominations that be done in the midst thereof," Tertullian says the mark is the letter Tau, *i.e.* T, "a kind of Cross, which (it was foretold) was to be in our foreheads in the True Catholic Jerusalem[3]."

The use of the Cross in Baptism has already been alluded to, see p. 57 § 2.

[1] Ad omnem progressum atque promotum, ad omnem aditum et exitum, ad vestitum et calciatum, ad lavacra, ad mensas, ad lumina, ad cubilia, ad sedilia, quacumque nos conversatio exercet, frontem signaculo terimus.

[2] Latebisne tu cum lectulum cum corpusculum tuum signas?

[3] Illa nota scilicet de qua Ezechiel: Dicit Dominus ad me, Pertransi in medio portae in media Hierusalem, et da signum Tau in frontibus virorum. Ipsa est enim littera graecorum Tau, nostra autem T, species crucis, quam...futuram in frontibus nostris apud veram et catholicam Hierusalem, &c. [Prof. Barnes writes:—The Hebrew is "Thou shalt set a *Tau*" *i.e.* the letter Tau, which anciently had the form X—καὶ σημειώσεις τὸ θαῦ is the rendering of Aquila and Herodion.]

Prayer was offered, with hands outstretched in sign of the Cross, both publicly and privately, standing or kneeling, but not sitting[1].

§ x. *The Jews in North Africa.*

As has been already remarked[2] the Jews were present in large numbers throughout North Africa, and especially in Carthage, at the end of the second century. Though at first they seem to have lived on good terms with the Christian community after the destruction of Jerusalem—this is implied in their use of common cemeteries—by Tertullian's time they had shewn themselves in Carthage as elsewhere its most bitter opponents. Thus we read in the *Apology*, " all outside the Church are her enemies, and especially Jews on account of their jealousy of us[3]." This spirit of opposition was recognized and met by frequent " Apologies " on the Christian side, of which perhaps the best known is Justin Martyr's " Dialogue with Trypho the Jew," which belongs to the middle of the second century.

Tertullian, as we might expect, is not slow to defend the Faith, and as usual carries the war into the enemy's camp. For instance, when speaking of the Christian

---

[1] See above, § 5, p. 85.

[2] See Chap. II. pp. 11, 27.

[3] Tot hostes ejus quot extranei, et quidem proprie ex aemulatione Judaei. *Apol.* VII.

belief in "One Baptism for the remission of sins," he contrasts with it the frequent ceremonial washings of the Jews, which he says are of no service. "The Jew washes every day, because every day he is defiled [1]"; and again, "although the Jew washes his whole body every day, yet he is never clean. At any rate, his hands are always unclean, stained for ever with the blood of Prophets and of the Lord Himself [2]."

Not very long before the publication of the *Apology* (197), a caricature of Christ had been paraded through the streets of Carthage, consisting of a human figure with ass's ears, one foot hoofed, carrying a book and wearing a toga: it bore the inscription, "The God of the Christians lying in the ass's stall [3]." The author of this caricature, Tertullian informs us, was "a vile creature who played tricks on wild beasts in the amphi-

[1] *de Bapt.* xv. Israel Judaeus quotidie lavat, quia quotidie inquinatur.

[2] *de Orat.* xiv. Omnibus licet membris lavet quotidie Israel, nunquam tamen mundus est. Certe manus ejus semper immundae, sanguine Prophetarum et Ipsius Domini cruentatae in aeternum.

[3] *Apol.* xvi. Nova jam Dei nostri in ista proxime civitate editio publicata est, ex quo quidam frustrandis bestiis mercenarius noxius picturam proposuit cum ejusmodi inscriptione : DEUS CHRISTIANORUM ONOKOITHΣ. Is erat auribus asininis, altero pede ungulatus, librum gestans et togatus.—Oehler would read, ὀνοκοιήτης, or ὀνοκοήτης, quoting Hesychius, κοιᾶται, ἱερᾶται and κοιής, ἱερεὺς Καβείρων, and rendering "asinarius sacerdos." Liddell and Scott translate "ass-worshipper." Minucius Felix refers to the popular belief that Christians worshipped an ass's head (inde est quod audire te dicis, caput asini rem nobis esse divinam. *Octavius*, xxviii.) and the *graffito* from the slave's room in the Palatine is familiar to all.

theatre for hire," and in the parallel passage in *ad Nationes* I. xiv. he tells us he was a renegade Jew[1].

In a passage in the *Scorpiace* he asks indignantly, "Will you set there—in the very presence of God— the synagogues of the Jews also, *which are the source of all our persecutions*, before which the Apostles suffered scourging? and with them will you set the peoples of the Gentiles, with their own special amphitheatre, where they shout at ease, Down with the Third Race of Mankind?"—the first race being the Gentiles, and the second the Jews[2]. He alludes to this name for the Christians also in *ad Natt.* I. viii. *Plane tertium genus dicimur*, "We are plainly called the third race of mankind": and again *ibid.* xx. where he says scornfully that the Gentiles also have their third kind of human beings, neither male nor female[3], *sc.* eunuchs. But elsewhere he disclaims this title as absurd: "Consider," he says, "whether those whom you call the Third Race, are not in possession of the first place: for there is no nation in the world which is not Christian[4]." He will

---

[1] Nova jam de Deo nostro fama suggessit, nec adeo nuper quidam perditissimus in ista civitate, etiam suae religionis desertor...Judaeus, &c.

[2] Illic constitues et synagogas Judaeorum, fontes persecutionum, apud quas Apostoli flagella perpessi sunt? Et populos nationum cum suo quidem circo, ubi facile conclamant, Usque quo genus tertium? *Scorp.* x.

[3] Habetis et vos tertium genus, etsi non de tertio ritu, attamen de tertio sexu.

[4] Verum recogitate, ne quos tertium genus dicitis principem locum obtineant, siquidem non ulla gens non christiana. *ad Nat.* I. VIII.

therefore not allow for a moment that Jews can be put on an equality with Christians.

As to the general relations between Jews and Christians, Tertullian speaks at length in the *Apology*[1], where he adopts this line of argument: We Christians base our belief in the one God on the warrant of God's revelation of Himself in the Jewish Old Testament Scriptures, which are among the most ancient documents in the world: we worship the same God as the Jews: but we differ from them in this, that we accept, and they do not, the Divinity of Jesus of Nazareth: we hold, they do not, that Christ is the Messiah foretold by the Prophets for the Jews: they misunderstood Him, His Advent, His work, and His doctrine, and put Him to death: but He rose again, and the truth of our claims for Him as against the Jews is shewn by the success of the preaching of the Gospel throughout the world.

Tertullian assumes throughout that Judaism is preparatory for the Gospel, and that Christianity is a development from, not the destruction of, the teaching of the Old Testament, thereby fulfilling the words of Christ Himself, " Think not that I am come to destroy the Law or the Prophets: I am not come to destroy but to fulfil[2]."

But the constant antagonism of the Jews was a difficulty to be reckoned with: and Tertullian sets

---

[1] Ch. xviii.—xxi.
[2] S. Matt. v. 17.

himself the task of specifically attacking the Jewish position, in his Treatise *Against the Jews*, which belongs to the period 200—206. It is a general opinion among critics that this work as we have it is not as the author left it: the first eight chapters may be genuine, but chapters ix.—xiv., it is maintained, are the work of a forger, who borrowed them from the third book against Marcion and from other sources. Monceaux[1] does not hold this view; and by a careful analysis of the line of thought gives good reasons for accepting the work in its present condition as Tertullian's own: he considers that the author himself borrowed his own arguments in *adv. Marc.* III. from his previously written treatise[2], and that this view is upheld by such a passage as the following: "It will now be possible for the heretic to learn clearly enough, *together with the Jew himself*, the reason for the errors of this Jew, whom he has taken for his guide in this argument: he has fallen into the same ditch, as the blind led by the blind[3]." And so, later, after transcribing a passage from *adv. Jud.*, he says, "Let the heretic now cease to borrow his poison from the Jew, an asp from the viper, as the saying is[4]."

[1] p. 297 *foll.*

[2] For dates of Tertullian's writings see *Appendix*.

[3] Discat nunc haereticus ex abundanti cum ipso licebit Judaeo rationem quoque errorum ejus, a quo ducatum mutuatus in hac argumentatione caecus a caeco in eandem decidit foveam. *adv. Marc.* III. VII.

[4] Desinat nunc haereticus a Judaeo, aspis quod aiunt a vipera, mutuari venenum. *ibid.* VIII.

Assuming then the authenticity of the work as it has reached us, we find that the occasion which gave rise to it, was a discussion between a heathen and a Jewish proselyte as to whether Gentiles could be saved: this seems to have taken place at Carthage and to have excited much interest; from his description of the details of the episode, it seems likely that Tertullian himself was present: at all events, he says that the dispute was left undecided, and so he deals with it at greater length himself in this treatise. In the course of it, he shews that it is impossible to exclude Gentiles from the mercy of God, for the Old Testament is constantly asserting that its covenant is intended for all nations. The Mosaic dispensation, with its rites of circumcision, observance of the Sabbath, and so forth, was only transitory, and finds its completion in the spiritual kingdom of Christ: the Messiah has already come, as definitely prophesied: the blindness of the Jews in refusing to accept these facts is due to pride and ambition. Let them take warning. The chastisement which has fallen on them as a nation since they rejected Christ, is a proof of the Divine displeasure and of the truth of Christianity.

§ xi. *Heresy and Heretics.*

At the end of the second century the Church had not yet reached that precision of statement about doctrine, which she afterwards attained. Men were still "feeling after" the Truth, if haply they might find it: and Truth is often best reached by clearly seeing what is Untrue. Consequently, the attempts made by the early Church to express the Truth have their special value, though they were often erroneous: and Heresy and Heretics, though themselves to be condemned, have done good service by acting as sign-posts, warning faithful enquirers off wrong paths. These teachers of erroneous views, with their misguided though doubtless sincere efforts to reach the Truth, were found in North Africa as elsewhere, and Tertullian attacks them with characteristic energy. Not to mention Montanus, whose errors Tertullian himself shared, and of whom enough is said elsewhere[1], there were several others, whose influence at Carthage was so great, as to call for special notice and correction[2]. Except in the case of Praxeas and Patripassianism, almost all Tertullian's polemics were directed against Gnostic heresies. These he dealt with incidentally in the course of his works published from time to time[3]: but he also attacked them specifically along two lines; (1) *generally*, by inveighing against the right claimed by heretics to maintain their views in face of the prescriptive claims of the Church; and (2) *specially* by treatises written against particular heretics.

---

[1] See Chap. VII.

[2] See Monceaux, p. 301 *foll.*

[3] See lower, end of this section, p. 119.

The *first* of these lines of argument we find followed in his Treatise *de Praescriptione Haereticorum*, written probably about the year 200. In this he raises a demurrer on behalf of the Church: she has a prescriptive right to the position which heretics seek to hold: she is already in possession, and has been there from Apostolic times: why should she surrender to those who only date from yesterday[1]? Heretics, he says, have no right to appeal to Holy Scripture: tradition is against them: what confusion is in their views! and so on. But it must be admitted that his arguments are really only such as to convince those who are already convinced[2].

Secondly, he attacks various Heretics directly under their own name.

MARCION was the founder of a sect, the Marcionites, who are generally reckoned the most aggressive, if not the most important, of the Gnostics[3]. He was born in Asia Minor, on the shores of the Euxine Sea, probably at Sinope : and appeared at Rome about 140, as a disciple of Cerdo, a Syrian Gnostic: by 144 he had openly separated himself from the Church, and

---

[1] *de Praescr. Haer.* XXI. XXII. XXXV. &c.

[2] It is to be noticed that Tertullian had anticipated this line of argument in *Apol.* XLVII. : and he recurs to it in *adv. Marc.* I. 1.

[3] It should be noticed that Professor Burkitt in his *Gospel History and its transmission* (ch. ix. pp. 289—323) protests against this inclusion of Marcion among Gnostics. The systems of Valentinus, Hermogenes and the rest he says were only half-Christian. "But Marcion's ideas were Christian through and through " (p. 291).

founded his own school, in which he sought to prove the irreconcilable antagonism between the Old and the New Testament: he taught that the God of the Jews was an inferior deity, Creator of the visible world, different from the God of the New Testament, and opposed to Him. The God of the New Testament sent Christ to redeem the world, who was however not the same as the Jewish Messiah, nor was He a true man, and He did not possess a real human body. To arrive at these results, Marcion had to make havoc of the writings of the New Testament, which he re-arranged, excised, or rewrote, to suit his own views. His chief work, *Antitheses*, had a wide circulation during the latter half of the second century, as is shewn by the many books written against it, by Theophilus of Antioch[1], Melito[2], Philip of Gortyna[3] in the East, and by Justin[4], Rhodo[5], and Irenaeus[6] in the West[7].

At Carthage, Tertullian found it necessary to pay special attention to this Heresiarch. The first edition of his treatise *adversus Marcionem* may be assigned to

[1] Euseb. *H.E.* IV. 24: Jerome *de Vir. ill.* xxv.

[2] Euseb. *H.E.* IV. 26.

[3] *Ibid.* IV. 25.

[4] Iren. IV. 6, 2: Jer. *de Vir. ill.* XXIII.

[5] Euseb. *H.E.* V. 13.

[6] Iren. I. 27, 4: III. 12, 12.

[7] In *de Praescr. Haer.* xxx., Tertullian tells us that later in his life Marcion was preparing to recant his errors and seek reconciliation with the Church, but was prevented by death from carrying out his intention.

the year 200, and has been lost: it seems to have been soon followed by a second edition, also lost: he probably published his third edition, Books I.—IV., in 207 or 208, Book V. between 208 and 211, all of which still survive. In this work he attacks and refutes Marcion's views in detail: in Books I. and II. he shews that it is impossible to separate the "Demiurge" of the Heretic, the Creator of the world, from the supreme Deity, the "good" God: in Book III. he shews that there is but one Christ, Son of the one God, the Saviour of all mankind, both Jews and Gentiles: in Books IV. and V. he accepts—for the sake of argument —Marcion's mutilated edition of the Gospel of St Luke, the Acts, and ten of St Paul's epistles, and then proceeds to disprove his theories. Incidentally, he shews that he himself accepts the Canon of both Old and New Testaments in practically the same condition as we receive it to-day.

The work of combating Marcion's dualism was clearly congenial to Tertullian : and though it cannot be said that he has solved the problem of the Origin of Evil, he has at least proved conclusively that Marcion's explanation of the difficulty cannot be right.

APELLES began by being an ardent disciple of Marcion, but after a time he broke away from him and founded his own school. Tertullian says that he himself wrote a treatise against the Apelleiaci[1], which must

[1] Sed quoniam et isti Apelleiaci carnis ignominiam praetendunt

belong to his second period, between 200 and 206 : but it has been lost. He makes several allusions to him and his teaching[1], whence it appears that Apelles held the Demiurge to be not really God, but an angel of superior rank; and that Christ, though possessing a human body, was not God Incarnate. Tertullian tells us that, after Apelles' breach with Marcion owing to his incontinence, he lived in Alexandria for some time ; and that on his return to Rome, "no longer a Marcionite," he fell under the influence of a certain virgin named Philumena in whom was "an angel of seduction" who pretended "to be an angel of light," and that it was owing to her miracles and visions that Apelles started a new heresy[2]. Tertullian exposes him and his character to unmeasured contempt.

VALENTINUS, a native of Egypt, the home of Gnosticism, was a contemporary of Marcion, and taught at Rome under the Emperor Antoninus. His doctrine of Æons, or Emanations of the Supreme Deity, of whom Jesus and the Spirit were two, his Allegories and Genealogies, and the mystic character of his general

maxime...et hoc suo loco tractavimus. Nam est nobis et ad illos libellus. *de Carne Christi*, VIII.

[1] *de Praescr. Haer.* VI. xxx. xxxiv.: *adv. Marc.* III. xi : *de Carn. Chr.* VI.: *de Anim.* XXIII. and XXXVI. : *de Res. Carn.* V. &c.

[2] Providerat jam tunc Spiritus Sanctus futurum in virgine quadam Philumene angelum seductionis, transfigurantem se in angelum lucis, cujus signis et praestigiis Apelles inductus novam haeresin induxit. *de Praescr. Haer.* VI.

teaching, gained wide acceptance in the latter half of the second century, and though his influence does not seem to have been great in North Africa, Tertullian thought it advisable to publish a special Treatise against him, which belongs to the years 208—211. It is below the writer's usual level, and is indeed little more than a poor adaptation of S. Irenaeus' work "against Heresies" which is specially directed against the Valentinians.

HERMOGENES was a painter—probably of idols— who lived at Carthage in Tertullian's time, and interested himself in metaphysical questions. He maintained the Gnostic principle of Dualism in Nature, and passed as a disciple of Marcion: he held that God and matter are opposed to one another, and that matter is eternal. This was an especially *African* heresy, and taught as it was by a man who could be seen any day in the streets of Carthage, Tertullian deals with it at close quarters, and does not shrink from attacking his opponent in person. "If you can't draw," he says, "better than you argue, you must be the worst painter in existence[1]." His treatise *adversus Hermogenem* belongs to his second period, between the years 200 and 206, and is not only a serious theological essay, but also an amusing caricature of the character and teaching of the painter; he "is a heretic by

[1] Si tam rectas lineas ducis, Hermogenes, quam ratiocinaris, pictor te bardior non est. *adv. Hermog.* xxxvi.

nature, a turbulent fellow, who calls loquacity eloquence, impudence courage, and personal abuse the duty of a good conscience. Nay, his very painting is illegal (in a Christian: for he paints idols): he is always marrying, and turns God's law ("increase and multiply") into lustfulness, and despises the commandment (against idols) by the practice of his art[1]."

PRAXEAS, who must not be classed among the Gnostics, was a Christian "Confessor" of Asia Minor; he had suffered imprisonment for his Faith, and had come to Rome in the days of Popes Victor and Zephyrinus to denounce the Montanistic heresy. He had succeeded in obtaining its formal condemnation, but had at the same time preached heresy on his own account. So eagerly did he insist on the doctrine of the unity of God, that he identified the Father and the Son: he taught—to use Tertullian's words—that "the Father Himself came down and entered the Virgin's womb, Himself was born of Her, Himself suffered, in short was Himself the same as Jesus Christ[2]." Among his many disciples the best known is Sabellius, the founder of the sect which bears his name. It is possible

[1] Natura quoque Haereticus, etiam turbulentus, qui loquacitatem facundiam existimet, et impudentiam constantiam deputet, et maledicere singulis officium bonae conscientiae judicet. Praeterea pingit illicite, nubit assidue, legem Dei in libidinem defendit, in artem contemnit. *adv. Herm.* i.

[2] Ipsum dicit Patrem descendisse in Virginem, ipsum ex ea natum, ipsum passum, denique ipsum esse Jesum Christum. *adv. Prax.* i.

that Praxeas came to Africa to propagate his views: Tertullian's words[1] seem to imply this, and also that he had been convinced of his errors—apparently by Tertullian himself—and had signed a formal retractation of them, which was preserved among the archives of the Church at Carthage.   But he afterwards relapsed, and at a later date—after 213—Tertullian deals trenchantly with his teaching in the *adv. Praxeam.*

He writes as a fully convinced Montanist, and he doubtless attacks the heretic all the more vehemently, on account of the part he had played 30 years earlier in persuading the Church of Rome to condemn Montanism.   " Praxeas, at Rome," cries Tertullian, " did the work of the Devil in two ways: he expelled Prophesying and introduced Heresy: he put to flight the Paraclete, and crucified the Father[2]."

From the foregoing brief sketch of Tertullian's polemical works written against particular heretics, it will be seen that the orthodoxy of the Church at Carthage was exposed to dangerous attacks, especially from Gnostic errors.   But besides these treatises against Heresiarchs, we find that Tertullian is con-

[1] *adv. Prax.* I.

[2] Duo negotia Diaboli Praxeas Romae procuravit, prophetiam expulit et haeresim intulit, Paracletum fugavit et Patrem crucifixit. *adv. Prax.* I.

stantly refuting erroneous views of doctrine in his other works: for instance, about Baptism in the *de Baptismo* I—XV., about the nature of the Soul in *de Anim.* XXIII. *foll.*, about the Person of Christ in *de Carn. Chr.* II.—XVI., about the Resurrection in *de Res. Carn.* II.—IV.: LV.—LXI.[1] From such passages as these we may see with what keenness of controversy the deepest questions were discussed by the Christian community at Carthage at the end of the second century, and with what difficulties the Faith was surrounded.

§ xii. *The Doctrine of the Holy Trinity.*

This Essay makes no claim to deal exhaustively with the views of Tertullian and many aspects of his teaching have necessarily been omitted. But it seems right that at least allusion should be made to the importance of his contribution to the History of Dogma, as shewn by his careful definition of terms, and by his use of words chosen with a lawyer's trained subtlety and exactness. This is especially observable in his dealing with the Doctrine of the Blessed Trinity. His choice of words profoundly affected all succeeding Christian thought, so far as the Latin language is concerned: and Bishop Bull was even able to say this about him[2];—" Read only his single work against Praxeas, in

---

[1] See Monceaux, p. 304.

[2] *Defence of the Nicene Creed* II. ch. vii.

which he treats fully and professedly of the most Holy Trinity; he there asserts the consubstantiality of the Son so frequently and so plainly, that you would suppose the author had written after the time of the Nicene Council."

Tertullian's treatise against Praxeas has been already alluded to in the preceding section, and a passage or two may be quoted from it here, to illustrate Bishop Bull's words. Tertullian is attacking the "Monarchian" views of Praxeas, which he understood as implying that the Father Himself suffered: and in formulating what he conceived to be a more correct statement, he uses legal terms, which connoted ideas familiar enough to men of his own generation, but apt to become blurred and indistinct through the lapse of ages. Thus substance (*substantia*) meant "property," person (*persona*) meant "a being with legal rights," a "party," an "individual" recognized by law, with a certain position (*status*) or condition (*condicio*), and a nature of his own (*natura* or *proprietas*) which yet might be shared by others.

Bearing this in mind, we may appreciate more precisely what Tertullian intended to convey by the following words: "(Praxeas) thinks that the necessary belief in 'One God' implies that the Father and the Son and the Holy Spirit are One and the Same: whereas the fact is that 'the One' is 'the All' provided that the All are derived from the One, that is to say by unity of Substance ; and provided also that nevertheless there be preserved[1] the mystery of the providential order which arranges the unity in a trinity, setting in their order three—Father, Son, and Holy Spirit—three, however, not in condition (*status*) but in relation (*gradus*), and not in substance but in mode of existence (*forma*), and not in power but in special characteristics (*species*); yes, rather of one substance and of one status and power, inasmuch as it is one God from whom these relations and modes and special characteristics are reckoned in the name of Father and of Son and of Holy Spirit[2]."

There is another passage in which he speaks of the mysterious relationship between the Father and the Son : " We shew reason why not two Gods or two Lords are spoken of, and yet Father and Son are two ; and that not by separation of substance, but by arrangement, for we pronounce the Son indivisible and inseparable from the Father; not different in condition,

---

[1] From this point the translation is that of Mr Bethune Baker, *Introduction to the Early History of Christian Doctrine*, p. 140.

[2] *Adv. Prax.* ii.   Unicum Deum non alias putat credendum quam si ipsum eundemque et Patrem et Filium et Spiritum Sanctum dicat ; quasi non sic quoque unus sit omnia, dum ex uno omnia, per substantiae scilicet unitatem, et nihilominus custodiatur οἰκονομίας sacramentum, quae unitatem in trinitatem disponit, tres dirigens, Patrem et Filium et Spiritum Sanctum, tres autem non statu, sed gradu, nec substantia, sed forma, nec potestate, sed specie, unius autem substantiae et unius status et unius potestatis, quia unus Deus, ex quo et gradus isti et formae et species in nomine Patris et Filii et Spiritus Sancti deputantur.

but in relation: for although He—the Son—is called God when He is spoken of by Himself, yet He does not thereby make two Gods, but one, owing to this very fact, that He also has the right to be called God owing to His oneness with the Father[1]."

In another passage he speaks of God the Holy Ghost: "Where there is a second, there are two: and where there is a third, there are three. For the Spirit is third from God and the Son, just as the fruit growing from the shrub is third from the root, and the river flowing from the stream is third from the spring, and the point of the ray is third from the sun. Nothing however is held to be alien from the source whence it derives its special characteristics, and so the Trinity descending from the Father by coordinated and connected relations, is in no way antagonistic to the "Monarchy"—the idea of the unity of the Godhead—on the contrary it protects the condition of the Divine Order[2]."

[1] *Adv. Prax.* xix. Rationem reddimus qua Dei non duo dicantur nec Domini, sed qua Pater et Filius duo, et hoc non ex separatione substantiae, sed ex dispositione, cum individuum et inseparatum Filium a Patre pronuntiamus, nec statu sed gradu alium, qui etsi Deus dicatur, quando nominatur singularis, non ideo duos Deos faciat, sed unum, hoc ipso, quod et Deus ex unitate Patris vocari habeat.

[2] *Adv. Prax.* viii. Secundus autem ubi est, duo sunt, et tertius ubi est, tres sunt. Tertius enim est Spiritus a Deo et Filio, sicut tertius a radice fructus ex frutice, et tertius a fonte rivus ex flumine, et tertius a sole apex ex radio. Nihil tamen a matrice alienatur, a qua proprietates suas ducit. Ita Trinitas per consertos et connexos

Another striking passage is thus translated by Mr Bethune Baker[1]: "So the connexion of the Father in the Son, and of the Son in the Paraclete, produces three coherent one to the other. And these three are one thing (*unum*), not one person (*unus*); as it was said, 'I and the Father are One (*unum*),' in regard to unity of substance, not in regard to singularity of number[2]."

Mr Baker also quotes a valuable passage on the meaning of *substantia* from *de Anima* XXXII.[3] and refers us[4] to the discussion in the *Apology* (c. XXI.)—which uses less technical terms than meet us in the *adv. Prax.*— on the meaning of the word ΛΟΓΟΣ and the doctrine of the Divinity of Christ.

Enough perhaps has now been said to shew the importance of Tertullian's share in the history of the development of Christian Doctrine. Those who wish to follow the subject further are referred to Mr Bethune Baker's book already alluded to (*Introduction to the Early History of Christian Doctrine*, chap. X.) and to M. Adhémar d'Alès "*La Théologie de Tertullien*," ch. II. pp. 67—103, where Tertullian's views on the Doctrine of the Trinity are dealt with at length.

gradus a Patre decurrens et Monarchiae nihil obstrepit et οἰκονομίας statum protegit.   [1] *l.c.* p. 688, n. 2.

    [2] *Adv. Prax.* XXI. Ita connexus Patris in Filio et Filii in Paracleto tres efficit cohaerentes, alterum ex altero. Qui tres unum sunt, non unus, quomodo dictum est, Ego et Pater unum sumus, ad substantiae unitatem, non ad numeri singularitatem.

    [3] *l.c.* p. 140.   [4] *l.c.* p. 143.

CHAPTER V

NORTH AFRICAN MARTYRS

§ i. *The Scillitan Martyrs*

In the year 177, the Emperor Marcus Aurelius issued two edicts which completed and rendered more precise the famous rescript of Trajan to the younger Pliny, governor of Bithynia A.D. 112 (?). By the first he ordered generally the punishment of those who troubled the state with new religions[1]. By the second he condemned to death specifically those who avowed themselves Christians[2].

In that same year a terrible persecution befell the churches of Vienne and Lyons in Southern Gaul: and by the first year of Commodus, who succeeded his father M. Aurelius in 180, we find the same thing happening in N. Africa.

It seems to be now established beyond a doubt that

---

[1] *Digest* XLVIII. 19. 30 (ed. Mommsen) Si quis aliquid fecerit quo leves hominum animi superstitione numinis terrentur [*v.l.* tenerentur], Divus Marcus hujusmodi homines in insulam relegari rescripsit.

[2] Euseb. *Hist. Eccles.* v. 1. 47 : 2. 1 *seq.*

The Amphitheatre, Carthage.

seven men and five women from Scillium, a town of
Proconsular Africa, were martyred on July 17th, 180, at
Carthage for refusing to abjure their Christian Faith.
Their names are given in the "Acts of the Scillitan
Martyrs" as follows: Speratus, Nartzalus, Cittinus, Ve-
turius, Felix, Apulinus, Laetantius, Januaria, Generosa,
Vestia, Donata, Secunda. These "Acts" were origin-
ally written in Latin, and consist of the *procès-verbal*
of the trial before Saturninus, Proconsul of Africa, "in
the Consulship of Praesens (for the second time) and
Claudianus" (which should have been Condianus) *i.e.*
180 A.D.

The Dean of Westminster, Dr Armitage Robinson,
has published this Latin version of the "Acts," facing
a Greek translation, in the first volume of *Texts and
Studies*, No. 2 (1891), together with an exhaustive
monograph on the *Passion of S. Perpetua* (of which
more below). If his conclusion as to the date of the
Latin version and its priority over the Greek version
be correct—and there seems no reason to doubt it—
then in this vivid narrative of the faithfulness even to
death of these N. African Christians 20 years before the
close of the 2nd century of the Christian era, we have
the oldest Christian document of Christian Africa, and
the earliest specimen of ecclesiastical Latin. It is
true that Pope Victor, whose Pontificate at Rome
probably belongs to the years 189—198 or 199, is
called by S. Jerome the earliest Christian writer of

Latin[1]. But not a word written by him survives: only we are told by S. Jerome that he was the author of several pamphlets on the Easter Controversy and other questions[2], some of which at any rate were presumably in Latin: and from the *Liber Pontificalis* we learn that he was a native of Africa[3]. It is true also that fragments remain of a Latin treatise written by a certain Archaeus, Bishop of Leptis, on the Easter Controversy: and the painter Hermogenes of Carthage, whose doctrines are so violently assailed by Tertullian in the still extant treatise *adv. Hermog.*, seems from what is there said to have published his views in Latin.

But this does not affect the claim of the "Acts of the Scillitan Martyrs" to be our earliest extant specimen of Christian Latin. The scene is laid *Karthagine in Secretario*, "in the council chamber of the Proconsulate at Carthage." The presiding magistrate, the Proconsul Saturninus, at once commences the interrogation, and informs the twelve prisoners that they can claim the Imperial clemency by recanting their errors. Speratus, who acts throughout as chief spokesman, replies that they have nothing to recant: they

---

[1] Tertullianus presbyter nunc demum primus post Victorem et Apollonium Latinorum ponitur. *De viris illustr.* 53. See above, p. 28 n.

[2] *de vir. ill.* 34 super quaestione Paschae, et alia quaedam scribens opuscula.

[3] Victor natione Afer ex patre Felice (i. 1, p. 137 (1886), ed. Duchesne).

have been guilty of no breach of the law, either by word or deed. After further discussion, finding Speratus obdurate, the Proconsul, who evidently has no liking for the office of executioner, appeals to the other prisoners and tries to persuade them to give up what he considers their unreasonable attitude: all—men and women—remain firm. They are offered a respite of 30 days in which to reconsider their position and "come to their senses." They simply reply, "We are and remain Christians." There is no excitement, no posing for effect: only the simple dignity of conscious innocence, confronting the majesty of the Roman Empire in the confident assurance of Divine favour and assistance. They are condemned to die by the sword, and receive the verdict with the joyful cry, "Thanks be to God: to-day we become witnesses in Heaven[1]." The chronicler ends his narrative "and so all were crowned with martyrdom together, and reign with the Father and the Son and the Holy Spirit for ever and ever. Amen[2]."

Incidentally Speratus in reply to a question of Saturninus "What have you in your box?" says "Books and epistles of S. Paul[3]," from which we may infer that the canon of the Latin New Testament was already in process of formation.

[1] Hodie martyres in caelis sumus: Deo gratias.

[2] Et ita omnes simul martyrio coronati sunt, et regnant cum Patre et Filio et Spiritu Sancto per omnia secula seculorum. Amen.

[3] Saturninus Proconsul dixit: Quae sunt res in capsa vestra? Speratus dixit, Libri et epistulae Pauli viri justi.

§ ii.   *The Passion of S. Perpetua.*

The story of the Passion of S. Perpetua and S. Felicitas is one of the most attractive and charming as it is one of the most familiar of the episodes belonging to the early Church.   Briefly it is this: we learn from Spartianus that when Septimius Severus was in Palestine in the year 202 he issued an edict forbidding under severe penalties the admission of proselytes to the Jewish religion.   He also made the same rescript apply to Christians[1].   The effect of this repressive act was felt by the following spring in N. Africa.   There Minucius Timinianus was Proconsul of the Province, but he died before his term of office had expired and was succeeded by Hilarianus[2].   There is an allusion to this same Hilarian in Tert. *ad Scap.* iii. under whose rule the populace are represented as clamouring for the suppression of the cemeteries, which afforded legal status to the Christian community as a corporation recognized by the law[3].

It was no doubt owing to this popular disfavour, stimulated by the Emperor's adverse edict, that a

---

[1] Judaeos fieri sub gravi poena vetuit : item etiam de Christianis sanxit.   Spart. Severus, xvii.

[2] Hilarianus Procurator, qui tunc loco proconsulis Minuci Timiniani defuncti jus gladii acceperat.   *Pass. Perp.* 6.

[3] Sub Hilariano praeside cum de areis sepulturarum nostrarum adclamassent "Areae non sint!" areae ipsorum non fuerunt.   See above, ch. ii. p. 16.

party of five Christians, three men and two women, were exposed to the wild beasts in the Amphitheatre of Carthage on March 7th, 203. Tradition says they were brought to Carthage from a place called Thuburbo about 40 miles away; but Dr Armitage Robinson in his edition of the *Passio* (*Texts and Studies*, I. No. 2. 22) gives good reasons for doubting this: at all events they were country folk, at first arrested as catechumens, and then owing to their being baptized while under arrest in their village, transported to the capital of the Province for due trial at the tribunal of the Proconsul. There they were joined by their teacher Saturus, who seems to have voluntarily surrendered himself in order that he might not be separated from his disciples in their agony; and so he suffered with them, making a sixth victim. The others were a young married woman of gentle blood, 22 years of age, Vibia Perpetua, who was suckling an infant son, a slave girl Felicitas, expecting shortly the birth of her first child, her brother Revocatus, and two young men Saturninus and Secundulus: of these the last named died in prison before the actual day of execution[1].

The document, *Passio Sanctae Perpetuae*, which is the primary source of our information, is based upon the narratives assigned directly to the two chief actors in the drama, Perpetua herself and Saturus, and given in

---

[1] Saturninus in the shorter "Acts" is called the brother of Saturus.

their own words in the original rough but simple Latin: the introduction and conclusion are by a third author, whom the Dean of Westminster considers may have been none other than Tertullian himself[1]: at any rate Tertullian alludes to the event, as a well known and generally accepted fact at Carthage, in a treatise which probably belongs to the year 213[2].

The pathetic story is so familiar and has been so often told, that it is enough here to give summarily the heads of the narrative. After the editor's introduction, Perpetua describes in her own words her father's first visit to her, his earnest appeal to her to renounce Christianity, and his indignation at her refusal, followed after a few days' interval by the baptism of herself and her companions. This led to their being subjected to the horrors of the public prison which she vividly describes. In response to the suggestion of her brother, she prays for Heavenly guidance by vision, and then describes what she saw; the golden ladder reaching from earth to heaven, guarded at the foot by a terrible dragon and on either side by swords and naked weapons, up which she

[1] Monceaux however in his *Hist. Litt. de l'Afr. chrét.* vol. I. p. 84 scouts the idea, which he calls an idle theory (*vaine hypothèse*). On the other hand, Glover (*Conflict of Religions in the Early Roman Empire*, p. 324) assumes as a matter of course that Tertullian is the editor.

[2] *de Anima*, LV. Perpetua fortissima martyr sub die Passionis in revelatione Paradisi solos illic commartyres suos vidit.

climbed after and with the aid of Saturus, and at the summit beheld the Heavenly Shepherd in the midst of His sheep, surrounded by many thousands of white robed attendants: "in joined hands" she received from Him the wafer of cheese, made from sheep's milk, and ate it, while all around uttered "Amen": at the sound she awoke with the sense of sweet food still in her mouth. As soon as she had related this to her brother they concluded that there was "no hope for them further in this world."

Then her father pays her a second visit, and once more appeals to her in deep distress but this time with true affection: again to no purpose. Then follows the public examination before the Procurator, and their condemnation to be flung to the wild beasts.

A few days later in the middle of their common prayer, she suddenly remembers her young brother Dinocrates who had died[1], at the age of seven, from a cancer in the face. That night she sees Dinocrates in a vision coming forth from a dark place foully clad, pale, and his face disfigured with the open gangrene, hot and thirsty, vainly trying to get at the water in a font, whose rim was higher than he could reach. This vision filled her with grief and led her to pray for him with groans and tears night and

---

[1] Of course unbaptized and a heathen, and not a Christian as S. Augustine somewhat strangely assumes in *de Anima ad Renatum*, I. 10.

day; at last (to quote the Dean of Westminster's words) in a later vision she sees him, in answer to her prayers, cleansed, well clothed, and refreshed: only the scar of the old wound is to be seen. The rim of the font is lowered to the boy's waist, and he drinks water out of a golden goblet that never fails. His need was supplied and he departed from the water "to play in the manner of children with great delight. Then I understood that he was released from punishment."

Yet another vision was vouchsafed to her just before the day of execution, in which she had to fight as a gladiator with a gigantic Egyptian whom she conquers with heavenly help, soaring above him and trampling him underfoot: and so she understood that she was to fight not with beasts but with the devil himself, and that victory would be hers. "Such were my experiences up to the day before my execution, but of the execution itself let another write, whoso will[1]."

Then follows the vision of Saturus, "written by himself." He describes how he, and Perpetua by his side, seemed to be borne aloft eastwards by four angels, though untouched by their hands, till they reached a garden, divinely glorious, where they found friends who had already suffered martyrdom in the same persecution, and heard the united sound of many voices ceaselessly uttering "Holy, Holy, Holy" in

[1] Hoc usque in pridie muneris egi : ipsius autem muneris actum, si quis voluerit, scribat. *Pass.* x.

" Salvum lotum!"

presence of One like a man with snow-white locks and youthful face. After standing awhile before the throne, they pass thence with wondrous satisfaction, full of joy. They then meet a bishop, Optatus, and a presbyter, Aspasius, downcast and sad, because of strife that had arisen between them. Perpetua, here, as we are specially told, speaking Greek, and Saturus do their best to compose the quarrel; then after a vision of many other brethren and martyrs Saturus awakes, conscious of a sweet fragrance and full of joy.

Then with the statement that God summoned Secundulus from prison to His Presence, a martyr in will though not in deed, the compiler proceeds to describe the martyrdom of the other five. In answer to their urgent prayer, Felicitas gives birth prematurely to a daughter, and so is not excluded from their blessed company, as she must have been had she still been expecting her baby on the day of execution.

The scene is described in full detail: the day of their "Victory" as it is called arrives: we read how Saturninus was torn by a leopard and worried by a bear: how Saturus, after escaping his exposure to a bear, was so lacerated by a leopard that he was drenched with his own blood and the people savagely shouted "A fine bath ![1]"—how Perpetua, tossed by a mad cow, was so unconscious of pain that she could rearrange her torn tunic, then help

---

[1] "Salvum lotum !" Prof. Burkitt has kindly allowed me to reproduce a photograph taken by himself of the flooring of a bath-room at Timgad where these words actually occur.

Felicitas who was in worse plight than herself after her recent confinement, and ask wonderingly when she was to be exposed to the cow: how at last when the young gladiator, whose duty it was to administer the *coup de grâce*, faltered, she herself shewed him where to strike, guiding his hand to her outstretched neck. "O most courageous and most blessed martyr, verily called and chosen to enter into the glory of our Lord Jesus Christ!"

Such is the outline of this remarkable history, instinct with breath of life, fresh from the amphitheatre, so grand in its simplicity, so touching in its pathos, so full of the verisimilitude of actual truth, that one readily concedes its claim to be the authentic account partly of an eyewitness, partly of the martyrs themselves. But what chiefly concerns us for the moment is the vivid picture it gives us of the life of the Christian community in N. Africa at that time, their constancy, devotion, and zeal. Saturus was evidently an Evangelist of wonderful power, whom no difficulty could thwart, no danger repel: so entirely had he convinced this little band, drawn from all classes of the community, of the truth of his message, that they faced an appalling death not only without fear but with exultation. He himself, it seems, had not been arrested with them in the first instance, but gave himself up to the authorities, that he might suffer with his disciples. His missionary spirit is unquenchable. In the prison and even in the amphitheatre itself, he ceases not to preach Jesus Christ, and his last act before his death is to convert the Roman soldier Pudens, from whom he asks for the loan of his ring, and after he had dipped it in his own blood, "Farewell," he said, "and be mindful of my faithfulness[1]: and let not all this disturb you: rather be strengthened thereby": and so left to him a precious heritage and memorial.

Many incidents and allusions throw light upon the position, the hopes and aspirations of the Christians of the time, and upon their religious observances, their belief in prayer—even for the dead—their ardent faith, their enthusiastic devotion to the Person of Christ, their acceptance—of course not yet fully formulated—of the doctrine of the Holy Trinity. On the other hand, the cause suffered then as now from personal pique and the quarrels between leaders; we see a Bishop and a Presbyter endangering the peace of the Church and the spiritual progress of their people by their strife and rivalry: we see also the grave trouble introduced into a heathen family by the conversion of one of its members: Perpetua's father in his passionate appeal to his daughter represents himself and all her relatives as disgraced and in despair. It is clear that Christianity with its exclusiveness and large claims on the daily life and habits of its adherents excited popular scorn and hatred: and though the jailors can be bribed to lessen the rigours of captivity, and individuals here and there are kind to the wretched prisoners, they excite fanatical execration as soon as they appear in the amphitheatre.

[1] Or, following the Greek, Of me and my faithfulness.

Then we have traces of the mystery of the Eucharist, received by Perpetua reverently "in joined hands," and accompanied by the liturgical Amen of those present, while the "*Ter Sanctus*" song of praise occurs in the vision of Saturus in presence of the Almighty.

Throughout the work runs the tinge of Montanistic thought: it is only necessary here to mention the prominence given by the compiler, both at the beginning and the end, to the influence and authority of the Holy Spirit, and His work in the Church, the importance assigned throughout to ecstasy and visions, the use of cheese as a substitute for the bread of the Eucharist[1], the eagerness of the convert to secure martyrdom. Many of these traits are obscured in the Greek version and omitted altogether in the abbreviated "Acts" compiled for liturgical use: whence some (*e.g.* Monceaux, *l.c.* p. 81: Leclercq, I. p. 139) have concluded that there existed besides this Montanistic work an official orthodox edition of the Acts, fit for reading in public, entirely free from such taint of heretical opinions as we find suggested in our present Latin version.

Whether that be so or not, it seems preferable to regard our Latin *Passio S. Perpetuae et S. Felicitatis* as the original contemporary work written at Carthage for the Carthaginians, but afterwards translated into

---

[1] This we learn from Epiphanius was a special practice of the Montanists and gained for them the name Artoturites—eater of bread and cheese: cf. *Haeres.* 49 Ἀρτοτυρίτας δὲ αὐτοὺς καλοῦσιν, ἀπὸ τοῦ ἐν τοῖς αὐτῶν μυστηρίοις ἐπιτιθέντας ἄρτον καὶ τυρόν, καὶ οὕτως ποιεῖν τὰ αὐτῶν μυστήρια.

Greek, and also abridged in several forms for liturgical use especially on the Nones of March, the anniversary of the martyrdom.

"Such is this singular and original work, so rich in curious information and so precious for the historian, so remarkable for the exquisite simplicity of the story, the correctness of its observation, and the exact drawing of its characters.—In this little drama full of freshness and life, which is nevertheless a faithful copy of what actually occurred, is struck as it were a fresh vein of imagination and sentiment. This book, this simple chronicle written by some unknown saint for the purpose of edification, suffices to shew how much of artless truth and poetry Latin literature owed to Christianity[1]."

[1] Monceaux, *l.c.* p. 96.

It is worth recording that on April 13th, 1909, the writer had the privilege of being taken over the Musée Lavigerie at Carthage by Père A. L. Delattre of the White Fathers, who has done perhaps more than any one else living to stimulate interest in Punic antiquities and actually to unearth them. In March 1907 he had discovered fragments of a marble slab which when pieced together gave this inscription :

> + HIC SVNT MARTYRES
> + SATVRVS SATVRNINVS
> + REBOCATVS SECVNDVLVS
> + FELICIT" PERPET" PASSI NON. MART.
>   *   *   *   *   *   *

and this in its restored state now faces the visitor on his entering the museum (see photographs opposite title-page). Père Delattre in his pamphlet describing his discovery (*Découverte de la pierre tombale des martyres*—J. Poncet, 18 Rue François-Dauphin, Lyon, 1907) supposes that this memorial tablet was placed over the tomb of the martyrs during the fourth century, probably in the time of Constantine.

CHAPTER VI

THE RIVALS OF CHRISTIANITY

A STUDY of the Church in North Africa at the beginning of the third century A.D. would be incomplete without some consideration of those rival cults which at the time were exercising a potent influence over men's minds[1]. The old Theology of Rome, notwithstanding its wide claims, and the attractive magnificence of much of its ritual, was practically moribund in the eyes of all thoughtful men. But the principle of Theism or Pantheism which underlay it was still alive, and capable of new development and varied application. Hence the growth in the early ages of the Christian era of three important forms of worship, each of which from differing points of view was a formidable rival to the Religion of Christ, and at times threatened its very life. These were: (1) The cult of Isis, (2) The cult of Mithra, and (3) The cult of Caesar. The first two were religious

[1] The importance of the influence of Stoicism on the thought and conduct of the first two centuries of the Christian era, great as it was, need not be considered here, as it appealed not to the public generally, but only to a limited class of thinkers and philosophers. The subject is treated at length by Glover, *Conflict of Religions in the Early Roman Empire*, chap. II. etc.

in their origin: the third was political. Each deserves a brief examination for a right understanding of the Church's position at the time.

§ i. *The Cult of Isis.*

The cult of the Egyptian Goddess Isis seems to have exercised a strong influence on many minds in the Roman world of the first two or three centuries of the Christian era. In the tangle of Egyptian Religions, ever changing and yet ever the same through hundreds of centuries, it is difficult to gain a clear account of what Isis worship meant to the North African at the end of the second century A.D. But that here as elsewhere its ritual, its mysteries, and its sensuousness attracted many votaries, cannot be doubted.

The legend of Isis may briefly be told: she was the wife of Osiris, the beneficent deity who represented the life-giving energy of the Nile: her husband was slain by his wicked brother Typhon (or Set) the spirit of evil and the foe of the human race; and his body was cruelly dismembered and the fragments scattered all over the land: these were duteously sought and gathered by the pious sister-wife Isis who wandered over the marshes of the Delta for this purpose in her papyrus boat; the dead body was restored to life, and so Osiris is able to become the Lord of the world below, and the Judge of the quick and the dead.

To Isis is then born the child Horus (identified with Harpocrates), the pledge of the revivifying power of Osiris even in the nether world: Horus sets to work in due time to avenge his Father and captures and binds the tyrant Typhon: but the gentle Isis interferes, forgives the monster and lets him go free.

It is a pathetic story, which appealed to the emotions and stirred the enthusiasm of the warmblooded people of the East. In Osiris we find the counterpart of the Hellenic Prometheus with his passionate devotion to the best interests of Humanity: in the divinely gentle wife and mother Isis, we find an anticipation of those qualities which evoked the devotion of later ages for the Mother of Jesus[1].

Closely associated with Isis was the worship of Serapis or Sarapis, an Egyptian Deity summoned from his obscurity by Ptolemy I. at the end of the fourth

---

[1] This point is brought out with his usual wealth of illustration and suggestiveness by Professor Frazer in *Adonis Attis Osiris*, p. 348 *foll.* He says, " We need not wonder that...the serene figure of Isis, with her spiritual calm, her gracious promise of immortality, should have appeared to many like a star in a stormy sky, and should have roused in their breasts a rapture of devotion not unlike that which was paid in the Middle Ages to the Virgin Mary. Indeed her stately ritual, with its shaven and tonsured priests, its matins and vespers, its tinkling music, its baptism and aspersions of holy water, its solemn processions, its jewelled images of the Mother of God, presented many points of similarity to the pomps and ceremonies of Catholicism.... In art, the figure of Isis suckling the infant Horus is so like that of the Madonna and Child that it has sometimes received the adoration of ignorant Christians."

century B.C., in obedience, as he declared, to a divine revelation received through a dream. His statue was brought with great solemnity from Sinope in Pontus[1]; and he was formally identified in popular estimation with the revivified Osiris; the object of the astute king was to provide his new subjects in Egypt—both native and Greek—with a conception of the Deity which could appeal to both, and which both could readily worship; his experiment was crowned with complete success[2]. Isis and Serapis became a power not only in Egypt but throughout the Levant, reaching eventually to the utmost borders of the Roman Empire[3].

As early as B.C. 80 we find Sulla recognizing the cult of Isis as legal at Rome: thereafter the authorities made frequent but vain attempts to undermine its popularity: so unsuccessful were these attempts that

[1] The story is told at length by Tacitus : see *Hist.* IV. 87, 88.

[2] Latronne (*Fragments d'Héron d'Alexandrie*, p. 210) conjectures with plausibility that this story, connecting with a Black Sea town a Deity who had been worshipped at Memphis for 1000 years, is due to confusion between Sinope and a hill called Sinopion near Memphis and not far from the Serapeum at Sakkara, the cemetery where still can be seen the sarcophagi of the sacred Apis Bulls.

[3] Cf. *e.g.* Juvenal, VI. 526 f. Si candida jusserit Io, Ibit ad Aegypti finem, calidaque petitas A Meroe portabit aquas, ut spargat in aedem Isidis, antiquo quae proxima surgit ovili, *i.e.* in the Campus Martius near the Circus Flaminius, built by the Emperor Domitian. Even in Britain traces of this worship have been found from the Roman Wall to the Land's End. In a grave in the Isle of Man has been discovered a ring with the figure of Isis' companion the dog-headed Anubis. See Bigg, *The Church's task under the Roman Empire*, p. 40.

at last in 42 B.C. the triumvirs tried to conciliate
popular sentiment by erecting a temple in honour of
the Goddess. Henceforth, except for a short period
after the battle of Actium, B.C. 31, the white-robed
tonsured priests of Isis become a familiar sight in the
streets of Rome, and allusions to the Goddess and her
votaries are not infrequent[1].

Suetonius asserts that the Emperor Otho openly
took part in her rites[2] and also that Domitian escaped
in the disguise of a priest of Isis in A.D. 69, when the
Capitol was stormed and burnt by the Vitellians (this
however does not appear in the account given by Tacitus,
Hist. III. 74)[3].

Plutarch's treatise περὶ Ἴσιδος καὶ Ὀσίριδος, written
probably in the reign of Domitian, gives us much
information about the cult and the legendary story, and
the hold it had on the Egyptians: he points out its

---

[1] *e.g.* Catullus, x. 26 Volo ad Serapin deferri: Tibullus, I. 3, 23
Quid tua nunc Isis mihi Delia? quid mihi prosunt Illa tua toties aera
repulsa manu? Propert. II. 33, 3 Atque utinam Nilo pereat quae
sacra tepente Misit Matronis Inachis Ausoniis. Lucan, *Pharsal.*, VIII.
831 Nos in templa tuam Romana accepimus Isin: and IX. 158
Jam numen gentibus Isin. Dill, p. 565 n.

[2] *Otho*, XII. Sacra etiam Isidis saepe in lintea religiosaque veste
propalam celebrasse traditur.

[3] Suet. *Domit.* I. Irrumpentibus adversariis et ardente templo
apud aedituum clam pernoctavit, ac mane Isiaci celatus habitu
interque sacrificulos variae (*v.l.* vanae) superstitionis, cum se trans
Tiberim ad condiscipuli sui matrem comite uno contulisset, ita
latuit, ut scrutantibus qui vestigia subsecuti erant, deprehendi non
potuerit.

connexion with Sun-worship, and from it he emphasizes the acceptance of the Dual Principle of Good and Evil in the world, Typhon calling for reverence and worship as much as Isis and Osiris[1].

Mr Scott-Moncrieff, in an illuminating article in the *Journal of Hellenic Studies* for May 1909, shews how this treatise of Plutarch is permeated by Platonism, and how its author is only acquainted with the genuine Egyptian worship of Isis and Osiris, at second hand and through Greek spectacles. At the same time it gives us an accurate estimate of the Isis-Osiris cult in the Graeco-Roman world in the first century A.D. "The great popularity of Isis," he says, p. 80, "seems to have grown up in later times chiefly owing to the skill she was thought to possess in magic, which would naturally endear the Goddess to the superstitious and magicians. Isis was the great sorceress, the Goddess who had enabled Osiris not so much to overcome his enemy Set, but to overcome the power of death and bodily decay."

Thus while to the Egyptian "Osiris was at once his judge and the pledge of his future existence," and in him "centred all the ideas connected with the springing up of new life from decay and corruption: he repre-

---

[1] *e.g.* § 45 *fin.* εἰ γὰρ οὐδὲν ἀναιτίως πέφυκε γενέσθαι, αἰτίαν δὲ κακοῦ τἀγαθὸν οὐκ ἂν παράσχοι, δεῖ γένεσιν ἰδίαν καὶ ἀρχὴν ὥσπερ ἀγαθοῦ καὶ κακοῦ τὴν φύσιν ἔχειν. "If nothing can be produced without an antecedent cause, and Good cannot be the cause of Evil, it follows that Evil just as much as Good must have a nature and origin of its own."

sented the revivifying power in nature, and especially in man ": while " Osiris is the male principle in nature, he is moistness, the Nile, the productive power,"—on the other hand " Isis is the female principle, the earth, the receptive power," and in that character she appealed to the tenderest sympathies of humanity and especially to womanhood and motherhood. She counted her votaries by tens of thousands, and her worship must be reckoned among the most serious rivals to nascent Christianity.

That the worship of Isis was familiar in North Africa appears from several passages in Tertullian: *e.g.* *Apol.* XVI., where in arguing against the folly of accusing Christians of worshipping the Cross, he turns the tables on his opponents, and says they do the same[1].

In *ad Nat.* II. 8 we find Joseph identified with Serapis, and Isis given to him as his wife, under the name Pharia, as being Pharaoh's daughter[2]! Later in the same book she is spoken of as a queen of Egypt[3]. As the Goddess of agriculture, the Egyptian Ceres, she is said to have been the first to wear a crown of ears of

---

[1] Quoted above ch. IV. § ix. pp. 101, 102. The same ironical argument isused with different words in the parallel passage, *ad Natt.* I. xii, where similarly Ceres of Pharos, *i.e.* Isis, is spoken of as a simple log of wood.

[2] Et Phariam adjungunt, quam filiam Regis Pharao derivatio nominis esse demonstrat.

[3] *ad Nat.* II. xvii. regnavit Jupiter Cretae et Saturnus Italiae et Isis Aegypto.

corn round her head, after introducing them to mankind[1]. In the *Apology* Tertullian mentions her as having been expelled from Rome together with Serapis, Harpocrates (*i.e.* Horus), and Anubis, by the consuls Piso and Gabinius B.C. 58. These magistrates of course, as Tertullian says, were not Christians, but they wished to restrain shameful and idle superstitions: all four deities nevertheless had been reinstated with highest honours[2].

We find allusion to the yearly search for Osiris and the joy with which he is discovered as emblematic of the burial of the grain in the earth, and the joy of harvest, in *adv. Marc.* I. xiii.[3]: and the close connexion between Isis and Osiris has been already noticed.

The *locus classicus* for our information about this worship is the concluding scene in Apuleius' *Metamorphoses* or *Lusus Asini*, more commonly known as *The Legend of the Golden Ass*: Apuleius, himself a native of North Africa, born at Madaura in Numidia, naturally

---

[1] *de Coron.* VII. si et Leonis Aegyptii scripta volvas, prima Isis repertas spicas capite circumtulit.

[2] *Apol.* VI. Serapidem et Isidem et Harpocratem cum suo Cynoscephalo Capitolio prohibitos inferri, id est Curia Deorum pulsos, Piso et Gabinius consules non utique Christiani eversis etiam aris eorum abdicaverunt turpium et otiosarum superstitionum vitia cohibentes. His vos restitutis summam majestatem contulistis.

[3] Sic et Osiris quod semper sepelitur et in vivido quaeritur et cum gaudio invenitur, reciprocarum frugum et vividorum elementorum et recidivi anni fidem argumentantur. Professor Frazer in his *Adonis Attis Osiris* (p. 339 n.) quotes this with other passages in support of his statement that "the ancients sometimes explained Osiris as a personification of the corn."

appeals to us as an authority of special importance:
and while his treatise repels us by its want of ordinary
decency, there can be no question of his wish to stir in
men's minds a desire for better things, nor of the
genuine enthusiasm and conviction with which he
declares himself a votary of Isis, and describes the
care and devotion required of those who would go
through the prescribed rites of initiation to her
worship. It is perhaps hardly necessary to go into the
details of what Apuleius tells us of his experiences
at Cenchreae after the full analysis given us by
Professor Bigg (see *The Church's Task under the Roman
Empire,* pp. 40—46) and by Mr Dill (see *Roman
Society from Nero to M. Aurelius,* pp. 575 *foll.*). A
sentence or two however may be quoted from the latter
(p. 577): "The daily ritual of Isis, which seems to have
been as regular and complicated as that of the Catholic Church, produced an immense effect on the Roman
mind. Every day there were two solemn offices, at
which white-robed tonsured priests, with acolytes and
assistants of every degree, officiated[1]. The morning
Litany and Sacrifice was an impressive service. The
crowd of worshippers thronged the space before the
chapel at the early dawn. The priest, ascending by
a hidden stair, drew apart the veil of the Sanctuary[2]

---

[1] Tibull. I. 3. 31 Bisque die, resoluta comas, tibi dicere laudes
Insignis turba debeat in Pharia.

[2] Apul. *Met.* XI. c. 20 (795) velis candentibus reductis.

and offered the holy image to their adoration...There was much solemn pomp and striking scenic effect in this public ceremonial. But it is clear from Apuleius that an important part of worship was also long silent meditation before the image of the Goddess...Apuleius has left a brilliantly vivid description of the Festival of the Holy Vessel of Isis at Cenchreae, which marked the opening of navigation, and received the benediction of the Goddess...It was a great popular carnival in which a long procession, masquerading in the most fantastic and various costumes, conducted the sacred ship to the shore. Women in white robes scattered flowers and perfumes along the way," and so on. Again (p. 582): "The chief Priest at Cenchreae is evidently a great Ecclesiastic, bearing the sacred eastern name of Mithra. He has given up ordinary civic life, and has probably abandoned his Greek name to take a new name 'in religion.' Every day two solemn services at least have to be performed in the temple, besides the private direction of souls, which had evidently become a regular part of the priestly functions...chastity was essential in the celebrant of the Holy Mysteries, and even Tertullian holds up the priests of Isis as a reproachful example of continence to professing followers of Christ."

(P. 583). "It does not need much imagination to understand the fascination of Isis and Serapis for a people who had outgrown a severe and sober but an uninspiring faith. They came to the West at the crisis of a great spiritual and political revolution with the charm of foreign mystery and the immemorial antiquity of a land whose annals ran back to ages long before Rome and Athens were even villages...The lonely, the weak, and the desolate found in the holy guilds succour and consolation, with a place in the ritual of her solemn seasons, which bound each to each in the love of a Divine Mother."

§ ii.   *The Cult of Mithra.*

The name of Mithra goes back through many ages to the original home of the Indo-European Family. We find him mentioned both in the Vedas of India, and the Zend-Avesta of Zoroaster and Persia. In both Religions he was the God of Light and was recognized as the "Protector of Truth, the antagonist of falsehood and error."

It is unnecessary to trace the conception of his being and attributes as evolved in the Vedic Hymns, and the philosophical thought of Hindus and Brahmans; his picture is far dimmer in Sanskrit literature than in the Zend writings: his personality became much more marked as it travelled westward. Starting from the high tableland of what afterwards became Armenia, his cult appeared in Mesopotamia, and borrowed elements from the astrologers and magi of Babylonia: it then spread northward along the east coast of the

Euxine sea, and westward through Asia Minor and so to Europe.

Briefly the story of Mithra as expounded to the uninitiated by the Faithful was this: He is not the supreme God of the Zoroastrian System, but the vicegerent on earth of Ahura-Mazda (Ormazd) and the Protector of mankind against their enemy Ahriman, the spirit of evil. Though not identified with the sun, Mithra is the genius of celestial Light, and in later versions of his story the chosen and firm ally of the sun God. When fully developed, his myth represented him as sprung from the "generative Rock": so the Light of Day springs from the sky as out of a solid vault: a tribe of shepherds—though the events are imagined as happening before the creation of man—witness the miracle of his birth, and see him issuing from the rocky mass wearing on his head the Phrygian Cap, and carrying a knife and a torch. He clothes himself in fig leaves, and begins a contest with the sun, who is compelled to acknowledge his superiority, and the two enter into a solemn alliance never to be broken. Ormazd (the Sun) now commits to Mithra's care the mysterious Bull, the incarnation of Divine energy and fecundity, which first Mithra has to catch and tame, and then after its escape from his cave to kill, a duty which he undertakes with the utmost grief and reluctance. It is this episode in the Divine Hero's life which is most frequently represented in Mithraic art, and the figure, grasping the exhausted bull's nostrils with his left hand, while he plunges his sword into its side with his right, must be familiar to all who have visited museums of ancient sculpture: for so wide-spread throughout Europe did the cult of Mithra become, that votive offerings, and even temples with elaborate ornamentation in honour of the God, have been found in almost all localities. From the death of this Bull, however, sprang all that was useful for mankind in agriculture and in science : wheat from its spinal cord, and wine from its blood. Hence Ahriman the evil spirit, the enemy of the human race, tried to prevent these blessings reaching the world : and so we find that the regular accessories of Mithra and the Bull are not only the two torch-bearers, one on either side with uplifted and inverted torch, symbolizing the nascent light of Dawn, and its fading into darkness at eventide, but also the scorpion, the ant, and the serpent, fastening on to the genital parts, and trying to suck the life-giving blood, before it can execute its beneficent purpose. Mithra is thus the mediator through suffering between God and the world, and, ever victorious over the powers of darkness, conveys inestimable benefits on God's creation.

Mithra also appears as the Faithful Friend and Protector of mankind. Ahriman tries to destroy the newly created race by various devices: first by means of a protracted drought, which Mithra defeats by discharging his mystic arrows against the hard rock, and thence producing life-saving streams; then follows a universal flood, but Mithra teaches one man to prepare for it by building an ark in which he saves himself and his cattle: with equal ill success Ahriman tries to destroy Man by devastating fire: here too Mithra circumvents him.

Thenceforth, received up into Heaven on the Sun's chariot, Mithra continues to act as the Faithful Friend and Protector of those who need and seek his help. He demands of them perfect purity of life, and ascetic control of bodily passions: devotees were admitted after repeated lustrations and vigils by baptism and mysterious rites into the brotherhood of the order, and passed (so S. Jerome tells us) through seven degrees of initiation, answering to the seven planets, bearing the names in their several orders of Raven (*Corax*), Occult (*Kryphius*), Soldier, Lion, Persian, Runner of the Sun (*Heliodromos*) and finally Father[1]. To all such duly initiated members, who remained faithful to their vows, Mithra the ever victorious—"*Invictus comes*"—promised victory over their enemies and a glorious immortality: while by the voluntary contributions of the associates, carefully administered through responsible officers, "Brethren" were tended in sickness and their poverty relieved. It was however a Society only for men; there is no evidence that women were benefited by it in any way except incidentally.

[1] Cumont, p. 152.

With such a constitution, appealing at once to man's best instincts and ready to assist his temporal needs, it is not surprising that Mithraism spread rapidly and continuously throughout the Roman Empire, at a time when the insufficiency of the old Religion was being more and more recognized, and men's minds were searching for something better and more satisfying to take its place.

The chief propagators of the new faith were the soldiers from those regions where the cult of Mithra had taken deeper root, who as they moved about the empire took their Religion with them, founded temples, and dedicated shrines. To illustrate this statement, may be mentioned the fact that in the province of Pannonia the two cities of Aquincum and Carnuntum[1] each shew to-day the remains of several temples in honour of the God, besides numerous votive inscriptions. Aquincum was the headquarters of the Legio II. *Adjutrix*, formed originally in the year 70 A.D. by Vespasian, and recruited largely from Asia: in 120 A.D. it was established by Hadrian in Lower Pannonia and doubtless brought with it to this place " the oriental cult to which it appears to have remained loyal to the day of its dissolution." In A.D. 71 or 72 Vespasian caused the important strategic position of Carnuntum to be occupied by the Legio XV. *Apollinaris* recently returned from the East, and recruited from Asia and particularly

---

[1] Cumont, p. 46.

from Cappadocia, and so, fully impregnated with the cult and tenets of Mithraism.

But though soldiers were undoubtedly the most active agents in the dissemination of this cult, its rapid diffusion was also due to slaves, who following their masters moved in vast hordes from place to place: and to merchants and traders, who in pursuance of their business had to be continually travelling. Moreover at the end of the second century the Emperor Commodus (180—192) was formally initiated into the sacred mysteries, and so the cult of Mithra received an impetus which brought it into the foremost place in the competing religions of the time: and by the reigns of Diocletian (307) and Julian the apostate (362), each of whom specially honoured Mithra, his worship was almost universally recognized throughout the Roman Empire: further, monuments of undoubted Mithraic origin have been discovered belonging to the first four centuries of the Christian era in every province and in almost every town of importance from Babylon in the East to Hadrian's wall in the West, from Cairo and Carthage to Vienna and Cologne[1].

Although Mithraic remains have been discovered in Carthage, the cult was not so firmly there established

[1] See the map shewing the dissemination of the Mithraic mysteries in Cumont : and cf. the suggestive episode in connexion with the Roman garrison of Hadrian's wall related by Rudyard Kipling in *Puck of Pook's Hill*, p. 191 etc.

as elsewhere: it is not surprising therefore to find only a few allusions to Mithra in the writings of Tertullian, but they are made in such a fashion as to shew that the tenets of the religious system were widely known and thoroughly recognized.

In *adv. Marc.* I. xii. he is discussing the way in which the Natural Philosophy of Heathenism deifies the elements, *e.g.* Fire as Vesta, the Earth as the Great Mother, recurrent seasons as Osiris, and he proceeds: "The Lions of Mithra philosophically represent the sacraments of the (sun's) arid and glowing qualities[1]"; "the Lions" here seem to refer to the fourth grade of initiation into the mysteries (see Cumont, p. 152), or, according to another interpretation, to the great heat parching the Earth when the Sun enters the sign of the Lion in his yearly path through the zodiac.

Again in *de Corona*, XV. (*fin.*), we have an important passage in which Tertullian deals with the ceremonies of Mithraic initiation. He is urging the Christian soldier to refuse the garland worn in honour of the Emperor. " What have you to do with a flower destined to death ? You have a flower of the Rod of Jesse, on which the whole grace of the Divine Spirit has rested, a flower incorruptible, eternal, that fadeth not away; by choosing this the good soldier makes progress in his heavenly rank. Blush ye, fellow soldiers of Christ, no

[1] Aridae et ardentis Naturae sacramenta Leones Mithrae philosophantur.

longer to be judged by His standard, but by that of
some soldier of Mithra, who when he is initiated in the
sacred cave—really in the camp of darkness[1]—has a
crown offered to him at the point of a sword, in mimicry
of Martyrdom, and then put upon his head ; but he is
warned by an interposing hand to thrust it away from
his head, and transfer it, if it may be so, to his shoulder,
with the words 'Mithra is my crown.' After that he is
never crowned, and retains that custom as a mark for
his probation, if ever he be tempted away from his oath :
he is at once recognized as 'a Soldier' of Mithra[2] if he
throws down the crown and says that his God is his
crown. Let us acknowledge the wiles of the Devil, who
assumes as his own some of our Holy Rites, with the
express purpose of confounding and condemning us by
the faithfulness of his own followers[3]."

[1] Oehler quotes in illustration of this passage Paulin. Nolan. *ad
Pagan.* v. 112 Quid quod et Invictum spelaea sub atra recondunt,
Quemque tegunt tenebris audent hunc dicere Solem ? "What means
it that they hide the Invincible God beneath dark caverns, and dare
to call him the Sun whom they conceal in darkness ? " Also S. Jerome,
Ep. ad Laetam, Nonne specum Mithrae et omnia portentosa simulacra,
quibus Corax, Niphus (*query*, Kryphius ?), Miles initiatur, subvertit ?
"Does he not overthrow Mithra's cave and all the monstrous
imagery, whereby the Raven, Niphus (*query*, the occult ?), and the
Soldier receive their initiation ? "

[2] The *miles* was the third order of initiation : see p. 151.

[3] Quid tibi cum flore morituro ? Habes florem ex virga Jesse,
super quem tota divini spiritus gratia requievit, florem incorruptum,
immarcescibilem, sempiternum : quem et bonus miles eligendo in
caelesti ordinatione profecit. Erubescite, commilitones ejus, jam
non ab Ipso judicandi, sed ab aliquo Mithrae milite, qui cum
initiatur in spelaeo, in castris vere tenebrarum, coronam interposito

We find the same idea of the Devil as the originator of these mystic rites in *de Praescr. Haeret.* XL.: "The next question will be, by whom is the meaning of those things interpreted which lead to heresies? By the Devil, of course: whose business it is to distort the truth; who strives to copy even the very acts of our divinely appointed sacraments by the mysteries of idols. He too himself has some baptized, his own 'faithful believers': he promises that sins shall be put away by Baptism: and if I remember rightly, Mithra there—*i.e.* in his 'Camp of Darkness'—marks his 'Soldiers' in their foreheads. He celebrates also the oblation of Bread, introduces the symbol of the Resurrection, and ransoms the crown (of martyrdom) at the sword's point. Again he ordains marriage with one wife only for his High Priest[1]. He has also his virgins and his celibates[2]."

gladio sibi oblatam, quasi mimum martyrii, dehinc capiti suo accommodatam monetur obvia manu a capite pellere, et in humerum, si forte, transferre, dicens Mithram esse coronam suam. Atque exinde nunquam coronatur, idque in signum habet ad probationem sui, sicubi temptatus fuerit de sacramento, statimque creditur Mithrae miles, si dejecerit coronam, si eam in Deo suo esse dixerit. Agnoscamus ingenia Diaboli, idcirco quaedam de divinis affectantis, ut nos de suorum fide confundat et judicet.

[1] Tertullian interprets 1 Tim. iii. 2; Tit. i. 6, where the apostle orders that ἐπίσκοπος must be μιᾶς γυναικὸς ἀνήρ, to mean that if his first wife dies he must never marry a second: cf. *ad Ux.* I. 7. Also *supra*, p. 45.

[2] Sequetur a quo intellectus interpretetur eorum quae ad haereses faciant? a Diabolo scilicet, cujus sunt partes intervertendi veritatem, qui ipsas quoque res sacramentorum divinorum idolorum mysteriis

In a fourth passage he mentions the initiation into the mysteries of Mithra by baptism, *de Bapt.* v. : " For certain of the sacred rites of the Heathen, as in the case of Isis or Mithra, initiation is made through baptism[1]."

The attitude of Tertullian in his implacable warfare against idolatry faithfully represents the mind of Christianity on this subject: Mithraism on the other hand " sought to conciliate paganism by a succession of adaptations and compromises : they endeavoured to establish monotheism while not combating polytheism, whereas the church was, in point of principle, the unrelenting antagonist of idolatry in any form[2]." And herein lies at once the reason for the earlier success of Mithra against Christ, and his ultimate downfall : for at first, while both religions held up lofty ideals, that of Mithra was far less uncompromising and so for the moment more attractive to many. But when Christianity in the time of Constantine became the state Religion, and by its inherent superiority claimed men's allegiance, the days of Mithraism were numbered, and after a brief recrudescence owing to the favour and

aemulatur. Tingit et ipse quosdam, utique credentes et fideles suos : expositionem delictorum de lavacro repromittit : et si adhuc memini, Mithra signat illic in frontibus milites suos : celebrat et panis oblationem, et imaginem resurrectionis inducit, et sub gladio redimit coronam. Quid, quod et summum Pontificem in unius nuptiis statuit ? Habet et Virgines, habet et continentes.

[1] Sacris quibusdam per lavacrum initiantur, Isidis alicujus aut Mithrae.

[2] Cumont, p. 197.

protection of the Emperor Julian, it gradually dis-
appears as a religious system, leaving the ethics of
Manichaeus to take its place[1].

§ iii.   *Caesar-worship.*

The deification of the reigning sovereign was an idea
familiar to the emotional peoples of the East.   Divine

[1] It may be permissible here to transcribe Professor Cumont's
summary of the parallelism between Christianity and the cult of
Mithra.   (Cumont's *Mysteries of Mithra*, Eng. Tr., p. 190.)   "The
adepts of both formed secret conventicles, closely united, the members
of which gave themselves the name of 'Brothers.'   The rites which
they practised offered numerous analogies.   The sectaries of the
Persian God, like the Christians, purified themselves by baptism;
received, by a species of confirmation, the power necessary to combat
the spirits of evil; and expected from a "Lord's Supper" salvation of
body and soul.   Like the latter, they also held Sunday sacred, and
celebrated the birth of the Sun on the 25th of December, the same day
on which Christmas has been celebrated since the fourth century at
least.   They both preached a categorical system of ethics, regarded
asceticism as meritorious, and counted among their principal virtues
abstinence and continence, renunciation and self-control.   Their
conceptions of the world and of the destiny of man were similar.
They both admitted the existence of a Heaven inhabited by Beatified
spirits, situated in the upper regions, and of a Hell peopled by demons,
situate in the bowels of the earth.   They both placed a flood at the
beginning of history: they both assigned as the source of their
traditions a primitive revelation.   They both, finally, believed in the
immortality of the soul, in a last judgment, and in a resurrection of
the dead, consequent upon a final conflagration of the Universe."
The position of Mithraism in its relation to Christianity is admirably
summarized by Prof. Bigg in his Lectures *The Church's Task under
the Roman Empire* (pp. 46—59) and in Dill's *Roman Society from Nero
to Marcus Aurelius*, Bk IV. chap. vi. pp. 585—626.

honours were paid to " the great King " of Persia, and the refusal of the Greeks to prostrate themselves in his presence was an ever recurring cause of offence : the Egyptians adored Pharaoh as an incarnation of the Sun God RA: and so when the empire of Alexander the Great was partitioned among his generals, we find the Seleucidae at Antioch and the Ptolemies at Alexandria acquiescing in the divine titles and insignia assigned to them. The people were ready to acknowledge their conquerors and rulers as God incarnate : and the founders of the empire were not averse to using this tendency for the consolidation of their power. Julius Caesar, whether in the intoxication of success or by deliberate calculation, had encouraged an excessive adulation. He had his chair placed in the Capitol opposite to Jove, his ivory statue in the circus surrounded by the statues of the gods, and another statue in the temple of Quirinus with the inscription *Deo Invicto*. After his death he was acclaimed " *Divus* " by Senate and people, and a new sanctuary was erected in his honour.

The opportune appearance of a comet in the heavens at that time was held to confirm the popular belief that he had been received into Olympus. Octavianus his successor did not scruple to call himself *Divi Filius*, and so early as 29 B.C. the city Pergamum in Asia Minor actually established an Augusteum, in which the Emperor Augustus was worshipped with a ritual of fully developed ordinances and a college of duly constituted priests.

Even Horace exalts the Emperor to divine honours[1]: and Tacitus (*Ann.* I. 10) says of Augustus "Nihil deorum honoribus relictum, cum se templis et effigie numinum per flamines et sacerdotes coli vellet." The attempt of the mad Emperor Caligula in A.D. 40 to have his statue erected in the temple at Jerusalem very nearly produced a Jewish revolt which indeed was only prevented by the assassination of the Emperor. Suetonius tells us that Vespasian (VIII. 23) with bitter gibe when dying said, "Ut puto Deus fio!" The shout of the mob at Caesarea deifying Herod Agrippa I. as related in Acts xii. 20 f. is familiar to us; "It is the voice of a God, and not of a man!" It must have been this

---

[1] For instance, he says

> Sive mutata juvenem figura
> ales in terris imitaris, almae
> filius Maiae, patiens vocari
>   Caesaris ultor :
> serus in caelum redeas etc.
>   *C.* i. 2. 41.

And in *C.* i. 12 after saying (l. 17) that nothing is born from Jove greater than himself, nor does anything exist like him *or second to* him, though Pallas comes nearest; in a later stanza of the same ode (l. 49) he yet can say

> Gentis humanae Pater atque custos,
> orte Saturno, tibi cura magni
> Caesaris fatis data: *Tu secundo*
>   *Caesare regnes.*

So *C.* iii. 5. 1.

> Caelo tonantem credidimus Jovem
> regnare: praesens Divus habebitur
> Augustus, adjectis Britannis
>   imperio gravibusque Persis.

thought which gave the sting to the Jews' words addressed to Pilate (S. Joh. xi. 50), "If thou let this man go, thou art not Caesar's friend." The Procurator could not make light of a claim not merely to kingship but also to Divinity. For by the time of our Lord's death the recognition of the Caesar cult had become part of the regular scheme of policy for the unification of the Roman Empire.

The idea seems to have taken shape in the time of Julius Caesar, and to have been acted upon by both Augustus and Tiberius; by the time of Domitian it was a marked feature of the imperial policy. That this policy meant the deification of the power of the people in the person of the reigning Emperor has been sufficiently shewn by Sir William Ramsay in his *Church in the Roman Empire* and elsewhere. In particular, in his *Letters to the Seven Churches* (p. 310), in dealing with the Letter to the Church of Pergamum (where as already stated the temple in honour of Octavianus had been set up in B.C. 29), Professor Ramsay goes so far as to suggest that the "new name" to be written on the white stone "and given to him that overcometh, and known to no one but to him who receiveth it" (Apoc. ii. 17) is purposely mentioned in contrast with the new name—Augustus—given to him who was worshipped among the Pergamenians "where Satan dwelleth" (v. 13). Professor Findlay in his edition of the Epistles to the Thessalonians (note on

2 Thess. ii. 4, p. 171 *foll.*) accepts the theory that the spirit of Antichrist "who opposeth and exalteth himself above all that is called God or that is worshipped : so that he as God sitteth in the temple of God, shewing himself that he is God," is found in the cult of the Emperor ; and that in this passage S. Paul had particularly in mind Caligula's mad attempt of some 10 years before. Like S. John with the prescience of a seer he foresaw what actually came to pass in the second century, that the worship of the Emperor was to be made the test of fidelity to Christ: and the same fact is recognized by Professor Swete both in his notes on Apoc. xiii. 4, 8, 14 and elsewhere.

It is remarkable that with the exception of the attempt of Caligula, mentioned above, the Romans were most careful to respect the scruples of the Jews as a nation, and did not force this Caesar cult upon them. When the legions entered Jerusalem, they were not even allowed to bring their eagles with them, but had to leave them at Caesarea. Neither oath nor sacrifice was exacted from them : even under Septimius Severus and his son Caracalla they were allowed to assume office in the government of the state, without doing any violence to their religious scruples[1].

The treatment of Christians was very different.

---

[1] *Digest* L. 2. 3. Eis qui Judaicam superstitionem sequuntur D. Severus et Antoninus honores adipisci permiserunt, sed et neces-sitates eis imposuerunt quae superstitionem eorum non laederent.

Even Trajan directs Pliny, governor of Bithynia, to meet their refusal to burn incense in presence of the statue of the Emperor with death. In the middle of the second century, S. Polycarp, summoned by the Proconsul of Smyrna to save his life by the oath, "swear by the genius of the Emperor and curse Christ," replied " How can I curse Christ who for 86 years has loaded me with blessings ? " and was forthwith dragged off to execution.

This cruel treatment of Christians was especially noticeable in North Africa. The martyrs of Scillium (see chap. v. § i.) were bidden by the Proconsul Saturninus to burn incense in honour of the genius of the Emperor. " We have done no evil, and spoken no evil " was the reply : . " we respect, fear, venerate our Emperor, for whom we offer prayer and praise every day." " We too are religious," replied Saturninus ; " our religion is simple : we swear by the genius of the Emperor, our master, and offer prayers for his safety. Do the same." " I refuse to acknowledge the power of the world," said another confessor, " I know only the Lord God, Emperor of all princes and peoples." They refused to sacrifice and were executed.

The same test is demanded of S. Perpetua and her companions and similarly refused (see chap. v. § ii.): and it is against this demand that Tertullian enters his most vigorous and eloquent protests. He deals with the whole question of Caesar worship at length in *Apol.*

11—2

XXVIII.—XXXVI.: he starts by saying that it is not strange to find the Romans honouring Caesar more than the gods: for a living Emperor is better than a dead demon. " You are more ready to perjure yourselves by all the gods than by the single genius of Caesar[1]." He claims credit on the contrary for the loyal fidelity of Christians, who make a practice of praying regularly for the welfare of the Emperor, in accordance with the directions of their religion. He commends the Emperor to the keeping of the supreme God, and by that very fact subjects the one to the other : he cannot put them on an equality, for, " I refuse to call the Emperor God, either because I cannot lie, or because I do not dare to mock him, or because not even he himself wishes to be called God[2]." He cannot be both God and Emperor at one and the same time : he must cease to be man, in other words he must die, before he can assume divinity; and he is not always ready to do this. Tertullian has the same thought elsewhere : " We do not admit the Emperor's divinity : as to that, as the saying is, we make a grimace. But you who say that Caesar is God, both mock him, because you say what is not true, and speak injuriously of him, because he does

---

[1] Citius denique apud vos per omnes Deos quam per unum genium Caesaris pejeratur. *Apol.* xxviii.

[2] Subjicio autem cui non adaequo : non enim Deum imperatorem dicam, vel quia mentiri nescio, vel quia illum deridere non audeo, vel quia nec ipse se Deum volet dici. *Apol.* xxxiii.

not wish what you say to come true: for he would rather go on living than become a God[1]."

If Christians had contented themselves with Tertullian's "grimace" at the Emperor worship, and had not felt bound actively to oppose it, they might have been left alone. But that could not be. The policy of the Roman government had been to extend the widest liberty of worship to all existing religions: they interfered with no local cult: and herein no doubt lay the chief strength of the *Pax Romana*. But they did insist on the universal recognition of the supremacy of the empire, as centralized in the person of the Emperor: and they made Caesar-worship the test of loyalty. This the Christian conscience could not allow; the consequence was that their community laid themselves open to the charge of disaffection, which they had to meet as best they could. Of all the rival religions opposed to their progress, Caesar-worship was the most persistent and the most dangerous.

---

[1] Non dicimus Deum imperatorem : super hoc enim, quod volgo aiunt, sannam facimus.   Immo qui Deum Caesarem dicitis, et deridetis dicendo quod non est et maledicitis, quia non vult esse quod dicitis, mavult enim vivere quam Deus fieri. *ad Nationes* I. xvii. *Cf.* Min. Felix, *Oct.* 21 Invitis his denique hoc nomen adscribitur; optant in homine perseverare; fieri se deos metuunt; etsi jam senes, nolunt.

CHAPTER VII

MONTANISM

ABOUT the middle of the second century after Christ, in the uplands of Phrygia, the home of the ecstatic worship of the Bona Dea with all its extravagances of devotion and orgiastic rites, there appears one of those enthusiastic "Revivals" which have periodically marked the course of Christianity as of other religions: we need only mention the names of S. Francis of Assisi, John Wesley, Edward Irving, and the recent Welsh Revivalists, by way of illustration[1].

Dissatisfied with the worldliness of the Church, and the laxity of discipline, in the year 157 Montanus a converted priest of Phrygia commenced a crusade, preaching against the prevailing licentiousness, and calling for a return to the vigorous faith and simple life of the early days of Christianity. His zeal and evident sincerity evoked much response, particularly among

[1] For fuller treatment see Monceaux, ch. vi. : D'Alès, ch. ix.: Bigg (*Origins of Christianity*), ch. xv. : Kaye, pp. 12—33 : Glover, p. 343 *foll.*

women, and he seems to have been always attended on
his peregrinations by two devoted "Prophetesses,"
named Maximilla and Prisca or Priscilla. As is so
frequently the case with emotional preachers, success
made Montanus lose his balance. He even claimed
to be the incarnation of the Paraclete, and that his
utterances and decisions should be received as the
divinely inspired revelation of God's will. He called on
his followers to break entirely with the world, to give up
marriage and earthly ties, to live in a state of frequent
ecstasy and vision, to court martyrdom. He preached
severest asceticism, and austerest living: he claimed
the supremacy of the individual conscience acting
under direct inspiration of the Holy Spirit, and denied
the rights of the community or Church to order men's
lives.

Such teaching was obviously subversive of the very
existence of Christianity, which by its essence ultimately depends on the society, and can only treat with
individuals through a fellowship: moreover the extravagance of these views could not fail to rouse the
dangerous hostility of state authorities. Consequently
the bishops of Asia Minor condemned Montanus and his
teaching, and excommunicated him and his followers.
Forbidden to reform the Church from within, Montanus
seceded and claimed orthodoxy for himself alone. He
called his followers *Pneumatici* ($\pi\nu\epsilon\nu\mu\alpha\tau\iota\kappa\omega$)—those
led by the spirit—as opposed to *Psychici* ($\Psi\nu\chi\iota\kappa\omega$)—

"natural[1]"—who were in his judgment a lower order of
aspiration and progress in the heavenly journey. The
schism soon began to attract attention outside the limits
of Phrygia, and famous bishops, Dionysius of Corinth,
Apollinaris of Hierapolis, Serapion of Antioch, were
drawn into the fray[2]. By the year 173 the controversy
had reached Rome, and Pope Soter himself is said to
have written a work against this new sect[3]: in 177, the
confessors of Lyons obtained from Pope Eleutherus a
condemnation of Montanism[4], but it was on the point of
being set aside by his successor Victor, when Praxeas
appeared on the scene from Asia, and the condemnation
was confirmed: apostles of Montanism, such as Proclus,
attempted to reverse this decision, but in vain: Rome
refused any countenance to the "Spiritualists."

Meantime, the appeal for stricter discipline and
asceticism and the claim made for more direct personal
revelation had attracted the ardent soul of Tertullian at

[1] 1 Cor. xv. 44, &c.

[2] See Eusebius, *Hist. Eccl.* v. 16. 10, &c.

[3] This statement is due to one Praedestinatus; but he is not a
thoroughly trustworthy authority.

[4] So Monceaux, p. 403: and the same view is taken by Dr Salmon
in *Dict. Christ. Biog. s.v.* Montanus (III. p. 938). But Professor
Stanton does not think that so much is implied by the words of
Eusebius (*H. E.* v. 3), τῆς τῶν ἐκκλησιῶν ἕνεκα πρεσβεύοντες. On the
general question of the change of opinion in the Church about
Montanism, which did not at first excite hostility, see Prof. Stanton's
Gospels, vol. I. p. 199, n. 2: and *cf.* also Irenaeus, *adv. haer.* III.
xi. 9.

Carthage. It is possible that he had come in contact with the Montanists while still at Rome. They were but a small body who favoured the new teaching, but as Tertullian was wont to say, one must look to the quality not the quantity of the faithful. In *de jejunio adv. Psych.* XI. he speaks of the force of his "inexperienced" few being greater than even the multitude of orthodox, so glorious as they suppose themselves to be[1].

In another passage he says "Your Church may consist only of three persons. It is better sometimes to avoid seeing your crowds of brethren rather than to reckon them up....Many are called, few chosen. Christ does not seek the man who is ready to follow the broad path, but the narrow: and therefore the Paraclete is necessary, who guides into all truth, who gives patience in all adversity[2]." So "where three are present, there

[1] Omnia autem ista credo ignota eis qui ad nostra turbantur, aut sola forsitan lectione non etiam intentione comperta, secundum majorem vim imperitorum apud gloriosissimam scilicet multitudinem Psychicorum. "But all this I suppose is unknown to those who are disturbed at our teaching, or has been discovered by mere reading perhaps (of the words of Holy Scripture) without the addition of the inner meaning, according to the greater forcefulness of our inexperience as compared with your most glorious crowd of Psychici," *i.e.* orthodox churchmen.

[2] *de fuga in pers.* XIV. Sit tibi et in tribus ecclesia. Melius est, turbas tuas aliquando non videas quam addicas....Multi vocati, pauci electi. Non quaeritur qui latam viam sequi paratus sit, sed qui angustam. Et ideo Paracletus necessarius, deductor omnium veritatum, exhortator omnium tolerantiarum.

is the Church, even in the absence of an ordained minister[1]."

These devotees were not necessarily excluded from Church membership: on the contrary we find a Montanist sister habitually seeing visions during divine service in church, which are regularly reported and examined afterwards[2]. The same fact—the presence of Montanist maidens in church—is implied in *de virg. vel.* XVII. in which passage mention is made of the vision of an angel to a sister prescribing the length of the veil to be worn during the Psalms or at any commemoration of God[3].

There was no open breach on Tertullian's part with the orthodox Church at any rate between 207 and 212, in which latter year he pleads the cause of all Christians and speaks in their name in his letter to the Proconsul Scapula. But after that date the alienation becomes more rapid and more marked. Even in 209, to which year is assigned his treatise *de Pallio*, his change of dress marks his wish to favour extremes, and to lead the more ascetic life: he gives up the flowing toga of ordinary citizenship and adopts the short cloak of the philosopher, which in the eyes of the public was

[1] *de exh. Cast.* VII. Ubi tres, ecclesia est, licet laici.

[2] *de anima*, IX. Est hodie soror apud nos revelationum charismata sortita, quas in ecclesia inter dominica sollemnia per ecstasin in spiritu patitur: conversatur cum angelis, aliquando etiam cum Domino, &c.

[3] Inter psalmos vel in quacumque Dei mentione.

always regarded as a symbol of asceticism: the pamphlet, a veritable *jeu d'esprit*, is nominally addressed to pagans, but through it all may be traced a covert rebuke to the laxity of the lives of professing Christians, and the call to a severer and sterner standard. He has not yet broken with the Church, but he is tending that way.

It may even be said that at a date previous to 209, *i.e.* even in 207, he was already a Montanist: for he gives a specific date for his first book against Marcion as the fifteenth year of the Emperor Septimius Severus = 207 A.D.[1], and a later passage is decidedly Montanistic[2]. But there were so many editions of his work against Marcion that it is perhaps hazardous to draw this conclusion.

By the year 213, the rupture is complete : even then he would probably have counted himself always orthodox : perhaps schismatical but never a heretic.— Always a fighter, always self-opinionated, it was not very long before he broke away from the Montanists himself : he founded an order of Tertullianists, which lasted for 200 years before disappearing, and is mentioned by S. Augustine[3], as still in existence in the fourth century.

---

[1] Ad decimum quintum jam Severi Imperatoris, *adv. Marc.* I. xv.

[2] c. xxix. Sed etsi nubendi jam modus ponitur, quem quidem apud nos Spiritalis Ratio, Paracleto auctore, defendit, unum in fide matrimonium praescribens, &c.

[3] *de Haeres.* 86.

In a paper read before the Cambridge Theological Society on Jan. 31, 1908, and published in the *Journal of Theol. Studies* for July 1908 (vol. IX. p. 481 *foll.*), Professor Lawlor of Trinity College, Dublin, protests against the view that the African Montanism of Tertullian was identically the same as the original Asiatic form. He maintains that Tertullian brought far more to Montanism than he found in it, and that his view of its teaching must have differed widely from the Phrygian type. He doubts for instance if Montanus really inculcated asceticism, though certainly Tertullian did: again, as regards martyrdom, though Tertullian encourages seeking it, the Phrygian position is not clear; under Marcus Aurelius and Decius the Asiatic Montanists seem to have been more anxious to avoid it than the Catholics. Professor Lawlor refuses to accept Harnack's words, who, following many other writers, has said[1] " what is called Montanism was a reaction against secularism in the Church." This may be true of the position of affairs at Carthage; but it is due to Tertullian much more than to Montanus.

[1] *Encycl. Brit.* xvi. 777.

CHAPTER VIII

THE "OCTAVIUS" OF MINUCIUS FELIX

WHATEVER may be the inner history of this treatise, and however difficult it may be to assign a date to it, there can be no doubt that it has a close connexion with the Church of North Africa early in the third century, and so it deserves our consideration.

Of the author, Minucius Felix, little is known. Lactantius twice alludes to him: " Minucius Felix," he says, "in the book called *Octavius* argued thus: that Saturn when he had been exiled by his son and had come to Italy was called the Son of Heaven[1]." Again, " Minucius Felix was of good standing amongst the lawyers. His book *Octavius* shews how apt a defender of the truth he might have been, had he devoted himself wholly to the rôle of Apologist[2]."

Jerome also alludes to him several times[3]. Except

[1] Minucius Felix in eo libro, qui Octavius inscribitur, sic argumentatus est: Saturnum cum fugatus esset a filio in Italiamque pervenisset, Caeli Filium dictum. *Divin. Instit.* I. 11. 5.

[2] Minucius Felix non ignobilis inter causidicos loci fuit. Hujus liber, cui Octavio titulus est, declarat quam idoneus veritatis assertor esse potuisset, si se totum ad id studium contulisset. *Div. Inst.* V, 1. 22.

[3] *de vir. illust.* cap. 58 (ed. Ben., IV. 2, p. 117). *Ep.* 83 ad Magnum (ed. Ben., IV. 2, p. 656) and in other places.

for these allusions, and what the author tells us in the treatise itself, he remains unknown to us, and this is the only work of his which is extant.

There are many little touches which shew his African origin: Octavius himself, it is implied, came from Africa (III. 4) where he had left his wife and children (II. 1). Another of the interlocutors in the Dialogue, Caecilius Natalis, is said to come from Cirta in Numidia[1], and it is worthy of notice that a series of inscriptions have been discovered at Constantine, the modern representative of Cirta, in which the generosity and civic excellencies of a certain M. Caecilius Natalis are commemorated[2]. The date of these inscriptions belongs to the year 210—217. Whether we may venture to identify the two names may be questioned: but the coincidence is at any rate noticeable: as is also the fact that the name of the author Minucius Felix occurs on a stele at Tebessa[3] and again in Carthage itself[4], while an Octavius Januarius is found at Saldae (*Bougie*)[5].

The author seems especially familiar with the

---

[1] Id etiam Cirtensis nostri testatur oratio (IX. 6), where Caecilius is referring to the orator Fronto, born at Cirta: called by Octavius "tuus Fronto" in XXXI. 2.

[2] *Corpus Inscr. Lat.* VIII. 6996, 7094—8, *Musée de Constantine*, pp. 76—7, pl. ii. (Monceaux, p. 475).

[3] *Corpus Inscr. Lat.* VIII. 1964 (Monceaux, p. 466).

[4] *Corp. Ins. Lat. supplem.* 12499, Minucius Felix sacerdos Saturni.

[5] *Corp. Ins. Lat.* VIII. 8962; Monceaux, p. 479; cf. "responsionem Januari nostri," XV. 2.

divinities of Africa; for instance, he refers to the Punic Juno, locally worshipped as Tanit[1], and to the African representative of Saturn, who answers to the Punic Baal: he says, "Saturn did not expose his sons, but devoured them: rightly to him were children offered by their parents in some parts of Africa, their cries being restrained by kisses and caresses, to prevent the immolation of a victim in grief[2]." Again, he mentions the deification of Juba among the Moors[3].

His style also shews imitation of the African writers Fronto, Florus, and Apuleius: while the parallelisms with the *Apologeticum* of Tertullian make it necessary to suppose one of three things: either (1) Tertullian borrowed from Min. Felix: or (2) Min. Felix borrowed from Tertullian: or (3) both used a common source. Of these three alternatives for many reasons (2) seems the most probable; and so the argument for the author's close connexion with Africa is strengthened.

As to the date of the book, the whole tone of the discussion points to a time of peace, without persecution, and various arguments lead us to find this in the interval between Caracalla (c. 213) and Decius (250) during which time there was only one short persecution of Christians by Maximin in 235.

[1] xxv. 9 Juno nunc Argiva, nunc Samia, nunc Poena.

[2] xxx. 3 Saturnus filios suos non exposuit sed voravit: merito ei in nonnullis Africae partibus a parentibus infantes immolabantur, blanditiis et osculo comprimente vagitum, ne flebilis hostia immolaretur.

[3] xxi. 9 Juba Mauris volentibus Deus est.

The treatise itself takes the form of the remini-
scence by the author Minucius Felix of a remarkable
discussion held in his presence by his two great
friends, Caecilius and Octavius, one day at Ostia, as to
the arguments used for and against Christianity.   The
setting of the scene is so delightfully arranged, that it
may well be a description of what had actually occurred.
The three old schoolfellows from Africa—for such they
seem to be—take advantage of a holiday in the law
courts to go out from Rome, one sunny autumn day, to
the beach at Ostia, where Caecilius kisses his hand to
an image of Serapis, and is gravely rebuked by
Octavius. After a description of the surroundings which
deserves to be quoted alongside of the famous opening
scene of the *Phaedrus*—we are told how they sat down,
Minucius between his two friends, under the shade of a
fisherman's boat, drawn up on the sand, and watched the
little boys from Ostia playing ducks and drakes with
oyster shells—Caecilius is rallied by his friends on his
silence, and says he had been thinking over the remon-
strance of Octavius; this leads him on to a biting attack
upon Christianity and the Christians.   It is the speech
of a special pleader and savours of the law courts; but
nevertheless it gives us a vivid picture—on precisely
the same lines as Tertullian's *Apology*—of the estimate
formed of Christians by popular opinion in the Roman
Empire and particularly in North Africa at the beginning of the third century. He accuses them of
being a congeries of ignorant rabble, largely composed

of credulous women, a folk skulking in darkness and avoiding the light of day, in public mute, but full of chatter in secret[1], they ostentatiously despise and reject the gods, and refuse to join in the popular religious services and public functions; they live apart, and give colour to the foul charges brought against them,—of human sacrifices, incestuous orgies, the worship of an ass's head or a criminal or a cross,—by the mysterious secrecy of their rites. (IX. 1—7.) "It is an old wives' superstition and the destruction of all true religion." (XIII. 5.)

Octavius, as a Christian converted from Heathenism, replies point by point: but like Caecilius, as a lawyer rather than a professed apologist: his defence is a mosaic of ideas borrowed freely not only from Tertullian's *Apology* but also from such writers as Cicero (*De Natura Deorum*), Seneca and Apuleius: he avoids dogma, and never even alludes to Original Sin, Redemption, the work of the Messiah, the Old and New Testaments; he makes no mention of the Person of Christ, the doctrine of the Trinity, Baptism, or the Lord's Supper: but dwells only on the three points of the Unity of the Godhead, Resurrection, and Recompense hereafter[2]. He addresses himself solely—as a matter of fact—to the literary philosophers of the day, and the

---

[1] Latebrosa et lucifuga natio, in publicum muta, in angulis garrula (VIII. 4).

[2] Monceaux, p. 492.

book is so far as it goes a defence of Deism rather than of Christianity. Nevertheless it throws much light on the popular estimate of the new Religion: and although we may feel that the strength of Octavius' arguments is not commensurate with the rapidity and completeness of Caecilius' conversion, yet the treatise as a whole attracts us by the lucidity of its style as compared with that of Tertullian, and by the value of its contents.

Note. The *Octavius* of Minucius Felix rests on a single MS. of the ninth century now in Paris: where it appears as the eighth book (liber *octavus*) of Arnobius! It is perhaps worth while adding here that a great deal of Tertullian himself rests on a single MS.; some treatises, *e.g.* the *de Baptismo, de Pudicitia,* and *de Jejunio,* on no extant MS.

CHAPTER IX

THE BIBLE IN NORTH AFRICA

THE martyrs of Scillium, A.D. 180, in reply to the Proconsul's question "What have you in your box?" said "Books and epistles of Paul the Just" or, according to another version, "The books of the Gospels, and the Epistles of the Apostle Saint Paul": the Greek version says "The books in use among us, and the Epistles of Saint Paul which follow them[1]." So early therefore as A.D. 180 we may conclude that considerable portions of the New Testament were circulating in a Latin Version among the Christians of North Africa: for Latin was the tongue employed by Speratus and his friends, and not Greek, nor Berber, nor Libyan.

Twenty or thirty years later we find Tertullian quoting from every book in the Bible in Latin, with the exception of Ruth and Esther in the Old Testament, 2 S. Peter and 3 S. John in the New Testament: it does not follow that quotations when repeated are identi-

[1] αἱ καθ' ἡμᾶς βίβλοι καὶ αἱ προσεπὶ τούτοις ἐπιστολαὶ Παύλου τοῦ ὁσίου ἀνδρός.

cally the same: and they often differ materially from the more or less stereotyped Vulgate of S. Jerome's time. They often also differ from the version followed by S. Cyprian 30 or 40 years after Tertullian's time.

How then are we to explain the existence and the variations of this Latin version in such early days? Obviously one of three theories must be true, or a combination of them: (1) Tertullian translated the passages quoted as needed from the original Greek; (2) he made use of an authorized version; (3) he made use of unauthorized translations of various books, and sometimes of more than one translation of the same passage.

There seems reason to think that (1) and (2) are both true: and herein we should find the answer to the question, Whence came the Latin versions used by the Scillitan martyrs? It seems probable that Christianity was introduced into North Africa originally from the East: but for the continuance of its life it must have been largely dependent on its intercourse with the metropolis of the empire. At Rome however we know that the Church remained almost wholly Greek, using Greek terms and customs and ritual, until well into the third century. How then could the North African Church have derived its Latin versions from her? There seems no alternative to the theory that they were produced, as needed, by local scholars in North Africa itself. Even Tertullian may have been

among the translators: and so North Africa has laid
all Europe and civilization under a lasting debt, by
giving us the first Latin translation of the greater part
of the divine library.

It is worth noticing that while Tertullian sometimes
uses different versions of the same passage in Latin, he
sometimes corrects the Latin from the Greek[1]. He
thus shews that he considers the " water of the spring
to flow more purely than in the wider river," while at
the same time he is prepared to admit that the Greek
itself is liable to corruption. And so we see that even
in Tertullian's writings the germs of literary criticism
are already apparent.

A comparison of Tertullian's quotations with those
made by Cyprian leads us to the conclusion that a
plurality of Latin versions was current in North
Africa, before the middle of the third century[2], and that
their source is independent of the text adopted by
Jerome in the Vulgate. This statement however must
be qualified so far as the Apocrypha is concerned:

[1] *E.g. adv. Marc.* IV. 14 Beati mendici—sic enim exigit inter-
pretatio vocabuli quod in Graeco est—quoniam illorum est Regnum
Dei. The Vulgate runs Beati pauperes: quia vestrum est Regnum
Dei (S. Luc. vi. 20). And again *de Monog.* XI. he appeals to what
he considers the true reading of the original Greek of 1 Cor. vii. 39,
ἐὰν κοιμᾶται instead of ἐὰν κοιμηθῇ. Sciamus plane non sic esse *in
Graeco authentico*, quomodo in usum exiit per duarum syllabarum
aut callidam aut simplicem eversionem.

[2] But see p. 182, note 2. Professor Burkitt doubts if we are
justified in drawing this inference.

Jerome made no separate translation of the Apocryphal Books: but the version incorporated into the Vulgate is identical with that used by Cyprian, and therefore African in origin[1].

If then it be true, as there seems good reason to suppose, that the Latin version or versions of the various books of the Bible—of which Tertullian saw the beginning and Cyprian the completion—as used by the Church of North Africa A.D. 200, were of native growth, it will readily be recognized how great was the importance of this earliest Christian Latinity, and how profoundly the efforts of the Church in North Africa influenced and affected all the literature that came after[2].

---

[1] Monceaux, p. 172.

[2] Professor Burkitt kindly allows me to add the following note: " With reference to the passage quoted from *adv. Marc.* IV. 14, the Cyprianic text of Lc. vi. 20 was (probably) Beati *egeni*, quia vestrum est regnum Dei. But Matt. v. 3–11, in the Cyprianic text, had *Felices* &c....It seems to me very doubtful whether Tertullian's peculiar renderings were due to anything else but his own renderings from the Greek. He translated each passage himself as he needed it directly from the original....The text of Nemesianus of Thubunae is not quite identical with that of Cyprian (see C. H. Turner, *Journ. Theol. Studies*, II. 602). But the *de Montibus* and the *de Pascha Computus* agree altogether with the Cyprianic text, which survives in the fragmentary Codex Bobiensis (k), first half of Matt., last half of Mc."

CHAPTER X

In conclusion let us try to summarize briefly the chief results of our enquiry.

We find that the Church in North Africa at the end of the second century of our era was in a vigorous condition, full of intellectual and spiritual life, well organized and well disciplined. Its chief centre was Carthage, its most prominent member Tertullian. But the influence of Christianity made itself felt throughout the Roman Province of Africa, and beyond its limits: and small townships like Scillium and perhaps Thuburbo contributed martyrs, whose names are still honoured and venerated by the Church at large.

We find a Canon of Holy Scripture both Old Testament and New Testament already in existence, and a Latin version or versions of nearly all the Books already in use.

We find the Christian community a strenuously active Corporation, not merely a Religious Brotherhood, but a Society for mutual aid, maintained by the voluntary contributions of its members, which are paid in every month to a common fund, and used for the support of its Ministers, and for charitable and other purposes[1].

We find indeed no building which can properly be called a Church, but meetings for worship or business are held at the cemetery (*area*), or in a private house, probably the Bishop's, which is sometimes called the *Ecclesia* or place of assembly.

The constitution of the community is organized on democratic lines: all baptized Christians can attend the meetings, and have the right of voting: they nominate their own clergy: and their influence in the decision of disputed questions is of the utmost importance. The position of the Laity in Church government is definitely recognized, far more so than is the case in the Church of England in our own times. But when once the clergy have been selected and ordained, the Sacerdotal Order, consisting of Deacons, Presbyters, and the Bishop in supreme authority, become a class more or less apart, and have certain privileges and duties assigned to them, which differentiate them from the Laity. The Bishop in particular is the ultimate source of authority; he commissions the inferior clergy to fulfil their various functions, and acting as the mouthpiece of the General Meeting, imposes or remits penitential discipline, arranges special fast-days, and presides on all occasions with a chairman's full power to initiate,

[1] See Monceaux, p. 395.

direct, and limit discussion. He is assisted by a Council of Presbyters, whose decision is final, provided it is in accordance with the words of Holy Scripture and the traditional teaching of Apostolically founded churches.

Each Christian community, while itself independent and free to make its own rules of conduct in non-essentials, is yet united to all the other churches by the acceptance of the fundamental articles of Belief. The essential unity of the Church is fully recognized through its many component parts. We find that the common ties uniting the various branches of the One Church are strengthened by mutual intercourse and by conferences such as we see already in existence elsewhere among the churches in the East. The example so set was soon to be followed by the Church in North Africa, and 50 years later, in the time of S. Cyprian, General Councils have become an established institution.

There are already the elements of a full ritual and liturgy in use: Public worship concentrates round the weekly celebration of the Holy Eucharist early on Sunday morning, and the details of this service seem to have been according to a regular order of Prayers, Bible-reading, and Preaching, followed by the actual service of consecration, at which only the initiated are allowed to be present. The service of Baptism, as the initiatory rite, seems to have become more or less stereotyped, and in most cases to have been followed at once by Confirmation. The Ordination of the clergy, and the Consecration of Bishops, seem also to have been according to a prescribed form.

The cycle of the Christian year does not yet contain the Festivals of Christmas Day, Epiphany, or Ascension Day, but recognizes Easter and Whitsuntide, and commemorates the "birthdays" of Martyrs, on the anniversary of the date of their death. Sunday takes the place of the Jewish Sabbath as "the Lord's Day": Wednesdays and Fridays are Fast-days.

The Christian community itself we find to be already a highly organized body.

The lowest rank consists of Catechumens—those under instruction for Baptism—and Penitents, *i.e.* Baptized persons or others who are under discipline owing to offences against the Common Conscience or the law of Christ: then comes the largest group, the "Faithful," full members of the Society by Baptism and Confirmation: some have special privileges, either owing to their suffering for the Faith as "Confessors," or to their special need, as "Widows" or "Virgins," who in return for the support accorded to them devote their lives to the service of the Church. Over all these Lay groups come the clergy, the threefold ministry as already described, and a lower Order of "Readers" (*Lectores*), answering nearly to our Lay-Evangelists who have received a special commission. Women are not admitted into the Sacerdotal Order, but, according to the Apostle's injunction, are bidden to obey and keep silence: the Laity also must under no pretext invade the functions and privileges of the clergy, except in cases of absolute necessity, which must always receive the approval of the Bishop.

The Doctrine of the two Great Sacraments is already clear: Baptism is not only the initiatory rite of Church membership: by it also is conferred the Forgiveness of sins. In the Eucharist we are taught that we feed on Christ, and Christ is made one with us, and consequently the elements themselves call for our deepest respect and veneration: they should be the first food with which we break our fast in the early morning.

The Discipline of Penance is remarkably severe, and readmission to Church privileges after a " lapse from grace " is only possible once, after prolonged and humiliating vigil and fast, and public confession. Private confession is unknown, or at least not mentioned.

The Christians themselves had many difficult problems to face in reconciling their profession of Faith with what was expected from them as citizens. So closely were the ordinary observances of every-day life connected with Idolatry, that it was hardly possible to stir abroad without having to conform to some custom, which seemed only right and natural to the Heathen, but was blasphemous in the eyes of a Christian. Tertullian as a Montanist adopted an extreme line; he would forbid Christians to serve in the army, to go to the theatre or amphitheatre, or to attend any of the public shows, to join any trade or profession which could be supposed to be even remotely connected with the manufacture of idols, or their worship. He even dissuaded the Brethren from holding any magistracy or public office, on account of the danger of being mixed up with idolatrous observances. It was this uncompromising spirit which caused the great unpopularity of Christians. Tertullian was doubtless an extreme type, but it is probable that there were many who sympathized with his views.

From the outer world the Christian community would not necessarily attract much attention, except for their abstention from many observances which to the ordinary citizen seemed innocent and commonplace. Their clergy wore no distinctive dress, and were generally occupied in some trade or profession in addition to their ministerial duties. Their legal position was assured as members of a Burial Club and Benefit Society : and they claimed to be good, loyal, law-abiding citizens of the empire. Nevertheless, if special circumstances directed attention to them, such as the jealousy of the Jews, or the hostility of a Proconsul or Governor, or the occurrence of some public disaster—a famine or pestilence—for which no immediate cause was obviously assignable, then the aloofness of the

Christians, their refusal to participate in the State
Cult of the reigning Emperor, and the mysterious
secrecy of their sacred rites, rendered them open to
the virulent attacks of the populace, and cruel persecutions recurred from time to time[1].

From without, Christianity had to face the rivalry
of competing religious systems, some of which, such as
the cult of Isis and of Mithra, counted their votaries
by tens of thousands in all parts of the Empire. Caesar-
worship, enforced by the Central Authority for political
reasons, was a serious danger to all who would not
conform. To the more philosophically minded, the
teachings of Stoicism possessed great attraction, and
deeply stirred the springs of conduct. The Jews
remained consistently hostile. In North Africa all
these influences were at work, and had to be taken
into account by those who were defending Christianity
or endeavouring to spread it.

In this connexion it is worth noticing that the
acceptance of the Christian Faith afforded the most
welcome escape for all honest minds—and to none more
so than to Tertullian himself—from what pressed as an
intolerable burden on the Heathen World, *viz.* the
Worship of Demons.

[1] The readiness of the populace to shout *Christianos ad leones*
may receive illustration from an amusing article in *The Times* of Sept.
4th, 1909 on "Cranks," which says "every great cause attracts cranks,
and suffers from them. No doubt there were cranks among the early
Christians, who provoked persecution by infuriating the average man."

From within, Orthodoxy was subject to manifold dangers. Various forms of Gnosticism arose, and their errors had to be corrected. The impossible claims of Montanism found in Tertullian himself a champion who has raised what might otherwise have been an obscure movement into real importance. We discern here the germ of much that bore fruit in many directions later on: A rigorous asceticism, which found vent in the austerities of the monastic orders; An assertion of the superiority of absolute continence in those who were striving after the higher spiritual life, which issued later in the enforced celibacy of the clergy; A claim for the direct illumination of the individual under the immediate guidance of the Holy Spirit, which led to many dissenting schisms. Tertullian's acceptance of such teaching resulted in his separation from the orthodox Church, which he attacked with all the bitterness and caustic humour that he had used before against its enemies.

It may be true, as a recent writer has stated[1], that his "polemics and his theological dissertations, his tirades against heresy, both before and after he became a Montanist, have turned to ashes: the modern man is weary to read them":—But it is also true, as the same writer goes on to say, that "his words still live: much of what he says might have been written yesterday:

[1] See an article in the *Spectator* of Sept. 7th, 1907 on "Tertullian and the plain man."

and the reader is again and again constrained to exclaim, How astonishingly modern all this is!"

We of the twentieth century have surely much to learn from the North African Church of A.D. 200. May the lesson she has to teach not be lost upon us. May we to-day draw inspiration and encouragement from the faithfulness, the constancy even to death, the discipline and obedience, the ready liberality, the wisely broad foundations of Church Government, the respect for duly constituted authority, and, last but not least, from the recognition of the supreme claims of Jesus Christ as the Incarnate Son of God, which we find so characteristic of the Church in Carthage at the end of the second century.

APPENDIX

CHRONOLOGY OF THE WORKS OF TERTULLIAN

FOR the convenience of the reader, it may be well to append here a list of Tertullian's writings with their probable dates. The scheme is transcribed from Monceaux (pp. 208—9), but it should be added that many of the dates assigned are quite uncertain, and some are disputed by other scholars.

FIRST PERIOD (before 200)

Before 197. *Liber ad amicum Philosophum.* Lost.

197. { *ad Martyras.* January or February.
ad Nationes (Bks I. and II.). After February.
Apologeticum. End of the year.

Between 197 and 200. } *de Testimonio animae.* After the *Apology.*

SECOND PERIOD (from about 200 to 206)

About 200. { *de Spectaculis.* After the *Apology.*
adversus Marcionem (1st edition). Lost.
de Praescriptione Haereticorum. After the *Apology*: after the 1st edition of *adv. Marc.*

de Oratione.
de Baptismo.
de Patientia.
de Paenitentia.
de cultu feminarum (Bks I. and II.).   After the
        de Spectaculis.

Between 200 *ad Uxorem* (Bks I. and II.).
and 206.   *adv. Hermogenem.*   After the *de Praescr. Haer.*
                 adv. Judaeos.
                 de censu animae. ⎫
                 adv. Apelleiacos. ⎪
                 de Fato.   ⎬ Lost.
                 de Paradiso.   ⎪
                 de spe Fidelium. ⎭

THIRD PERIOD (207—212)

207—208.   *adv. Marcionem* (Bks I.—IV.).
209.   *de Pallio.*
                adv. Valentinianos.   After the *adv. Hermog.*
                de Anima.   After *adv. Herm.* and Bk II. *adv.*
                    Marc.
                de Carne Christi.   After *de Praes. Haer.* and
                    Bk IV. *adv. Marc.*
Between 208 *de Resurrectione Carnis.*   After *de Anim.* and *de*
and 211.   *Carn. Christi, adv. Valent.* and Bks I.—III.
                    adv. Marc.
                adv. Marcionem (Bk V.).   After *de Resur. Carnis.*
                de Exhortatione Castitatis.
                de Virginibus Velandis.
211.   *de Corona.*
211 or 212. ⎰ *Scorpiace.*   ⎱   After the *de Corona.*
                ⎱ *de Idololatria.* ⎰
212.   *ad Scapulam.*   In the latter part of the year.

FOURTH PERIOD.   (After 212)

213.	*de fuga in persecutione.*
After 213.	$\left\{\begin{array}{l}\textit{adversus Praxeam.}\\ \textit{de Monogamia.}\\ \textit{de jejunio.}\quad\text{After the }\textit{de Monogamia.}\\ \textit{de Ecstási.}\quad\text{Lost.}\end{array}\right.$
Between 217 and 222.	*de Pudicitia.*

INDEX I. GENERAL

Adhémar d'Alès 76, 123, 166 n.
Afer, Africa 7
Altar 19, 78
Amphitheatre 33
Antichrist 162
Apelles 114
Apollinaris of Hierapolis 168
Apostolic succession 49, 50
Apuleius 6 n., 145
Aquincum 152
Armitage Robinson, Dean 125
Arnobius 6 n., 178
Artòturites 76, 136
Ascension Day 95, 186
Aspasius, Presbyter 133
Ass-worship 106
Augustine, St 5, 6, 131 n., 171
Augustus (Octavianus) 8, 159, 161
Aurelius, Marcus 24, 124

Baptism 46, 48, 54 foll., 157
Baptismal Regeneration 56, 63, 88, 187
Barnes, Prof. W. E. 104 n.
Belloc, H. 4
Berber 5, 8
Bethesda, Pool of 56
Bethune Baker, J. F. 121, 123
Bigg, Prof. 90 n., 141 n., 146, 158 n., 166 n.
Bull, Bishop 119
Burkitt, Prof. 112 n., 133 n., 181 n., 182 n.

Caesar, C. J. 1, 8, 159, 161

Caligula 160, 162
Callistus, Pope 90
Canon 179, 183
Caracalla 24, 34, 162, 175
Carnuntum 152
Carthage 1, 2, 22, 25, 27, 129, 183
Catullus 142 n.
Cherchel 16
Christmas Day 95, 186
Church (edifice) 18
Cicero 177
Cirta (Constantine) 1, 2, 174
Commodus 24, 124, 153
Confession (auricular) 92
Confirmation 57
Councils 51, 52
Cross, Sign of 57, 103, 104
Cumont 148 foll.
Cyprian 26, 38, 39, 51, 52, 54, 61, 70, 74, 76, 87, 185

Decius 172, 175
Delattre, Père 15, 137 n.
Demons, worship of 189
Didache, The 94
Dill 142 n., 146 foll., 158 n.
Dinocrates 131
Dionysius of Corinth 168
Divorce 95
Domitian 161

Easter 92, 186
Eleutherus, Pope 168
Epiphanius 136 n.
Epiphany 95, 186

Eucharist, The 45, 48, 70–79
Eusebius 113, 124 n., 168 n.
Exomologesis 88, 89, 92

Findlay, Prof. 161
Florus 175
Francis of Assisi, St 166
Frazer, Prof. 140 n., 145 n.
Fronto 174, 175
Fuller, Prof. 37

Glover, T. R. 130 n., 138 n., 166 n.

Hadrian 152
Harnack 172
Hell, Descent into 99
Hermas, "Shepherd" of 52, 90, 94 n.
Hermogenes 116, 126
Herod Agrippa I. 160
Hilarianus 16, 128
Hippolytus, Canons of 59, 60
Horace 85, 160

Inscriptions 12, 13, 15, 137
Irenaeus 94 n., 113, 116, 168 n.
Irving, Edward 166
Isis 101, 102, 139–148

Jerome, St 22 n., 23, 38, 39, 113, 125, 126, 151, 155 n., 173
Justin Martyr 44 n., 105
Juvenal 141 n., 142

Kaye, Bishop 22 n., 33 n., 166 n.
Kiss of Peace, The 76, 77
Kolberg 94 n.

Lactantius 6 n., 173
Laity, The 53
Lambessa (Lambèse) 3
Latronnne 141 n., 142
Lavigerie, Cardinal 15
Lawlor, Prof. 172
Lent 95
Liber Pontificalis 126
Lucan 142

Marcion 112 foll.
Marriage 95
Masinissa, King 8
Maximin 175
Mommsen 1, 6, 124 n.
"Monarchy" 122
Monceaux 28 n., 69, 89, 96, 109, 130 n., 137, 166 n., 168 n., 177, 182, 184
Moncrieff, Scott- 143
Montanism 36, 37, 136, 166–172
MSS. 178

Numidia (Nomades) 4, 8

Octavianus (Augustus) 8, 159, 161
Octavius of Min. Felix, The 69, 73 n., 103, 106 n., 165 n., 173–178
Oehler 76 n., 155 n.
Optatus, Bishop 133

Paul and Thecla, Acts of 63
Paulinus of Nola 155 n.
Pergamum 159, 161
Perpetua, St 14, 16 n., 36, 69, 86, 128 foll., 163
Plato, (Phaedrus) 176
Pliny and Trajan 67, 72, 124, 163
Plutarch 142, 143
Polycarp 163
Pontius Pilate 161
Praxeas 117, 118, 120 foll., 168
Prayer, The Lord's 81
Proclus 168
Propertius 142 n.
Prudentius 85 n.

Ramsay, Prof. Sir W. 15, 161
"Readers" 53, 186
Rebaptism of Heretics 52, 61
Renunciation at Baptism 56, 59
Resurrection of Body 33, 97, 99
Ring 60
Robinson, Dean of Westminster 125

Salmon, Dr 168

"Salvum lotum" 133
Scillium 125 *foll.*, 163, 179, 183
Seneca 177
Septimius Severus 3, 16, 24, 34, 128, 162, 171
Serapion 168
Serapis 140, 176
Soter, Pope 168
Spartianus 25 n., 128
Sponsors 58
Stanton, Prof. 168 n.
Stationes 94 *foll.*
Stoicism 138, 139
Suetonius 142, 160
Sunday 84, 93
Sun worship 83
Swete, Prof. 79 n., 87, 88, 162

Tacitus 141 n., 160
"Tertium genus" 107
Thamugas (*Timgad*) 3, 133 n.

Theatre 33
Thecla, Acts of Paul and 63
Theveste (*Tebessa*) 2
Thuburbo 129, 183
Tiberius 161
Tibullus 142 n., 146 n.
Timgad 3, 133 n.
Trajan 3, 24, 72
Tunis 4, 11, 25

Unction 57
Unity of the Church 59

Valentinus 115
Vespasian 2, 152, 160
Victor, Pope 28, 125, 168

Wesley, John 166
Widows 53, 86
Women, Position of 63

INDEX II

LIST OF QUOTATIONS FROM THE WRITINGS OF TERTULLIAN

ad Martyras ii. 68, 69.

ad Nationes
    Bk i. viii. 27, 107.   xii. 85, 102, 144 n.   xiii. 83.
           xiv. 107.   xvii. 165.   xx. 107.
    Bk ii. viii. 144.   xvii. 144.

Apologeticum
    i. 26.   ii. 72.   vi. 145.   vii. 11, 105.   viii. 73.
    xii. 29.   xvi. 83, 101, 106, 144.   xviii.–xxi. 108.
    xxi. 123.   xxviii.–xxxvi. 164, 175, 176.
    xxx. xxxi. 78, 85.   xxxvii. 27.
    xxxix. 30, 39 f., 67, 68, 79, 96.   xlvii. 112 n.
    xlviii. 33.   l. 32.

de spectaculis
    iv. 59 n.   xiii. 59 n., 70.   xx. 34.   xxiv. 59 n.
    xxv. 34.   xxix. 74.

de praescriptione Haereticorum
    vi. 115 (*bis*).   xiii. 98.   xx. 20, 49.   xxi. xxii. 112.
    xxiv. 115 n.   xxvii. 50.   xxx. 113, 115 n.
    xxxii. 50.   xxxv. 112.   xxxvi. 10 n., 100.
    xli. 53 (*bis*), 63, 73.   xlvii. 47.

de Oratione
    80–82.   iii. 75.   vi. 75.   xiv. 85, 106.
    xvii. 85, 86   xviii. 76, 77   xix. 19, 70, 78 n., 94.
    xxi. 18.   xxiii. 84, 94, 95.   xxviii. 19, 77.

de Baptismo
    i.-xv. 119.   i. 55.   ii. 55, 56.   v. 56, 156.
    vi. 56, 57, 58 *n.*   vii. 57.   viii. 57.   xiii. 58 *n.*
    xv. 60, 106.   xvii. 47, 48, 53, 54.   xviii. 58.
    xix. 64, 65.   xx. 65.
de Patientia i. 38.   xiii. 89 *n.*
de Paenitentia
    iv. 88, 89 *n.*   vi. 53, 88.   vii. ix. 88, 89.
ad Uxorem
    Bk ɪ. vii. 45, 156.
    Bk ɪɪ. iv. 70, 77.   v. 71, 104.   viii. 70, 95.
adv. Hermogenem
    i. 117.   xx.-xxii., xxxiv. 33 *n.*   xxxvi. 116.
adv. Judaeos
    109-110.   iv. 93.   vii. 27.   x. 76 *n.*   xiv. 78.
adv. Marcionem 112-114.
    Bk ɪ. xii. 154.   xiii. 145.   xv. 171.   xxiii. 70.
          xxviii. 58.   xxix. 171.
    Bk ɪɪɪ. vii. 109.   viii. 109.   xi. 115 *n.*   xix. 75.
          xxii. 104.
    Bk ɪᴠ. ix. 91.   xii. 93.   xiv. 181 *n.*   xl. 76 *n.*
de pallio 170, 171.
de anima
    ix. 70 *n.*, 170.   xxiii. 115 *n.*, 119.   xxxii. 123.
    xxxvi. 115 *n.*   lv. 130 *n.*
de carne Christi
    ii.-xvi. 119.   v. 36.   vi. 115 *n.*   viii. 114, 115.
de resurrectione carnis
    v. 115 *n.*   viii. 57.   ii.-iv., lv.-lxi. 119
de exhortatione castitatis
    vii. 18. 47, 48, 53 *n.*, 170.   xi. 87.   xii. 53 *n.*
de Virginibus velandis
    i. 96.   ii. 49, 51.   ix. 53 *n.*, 63.   xiii. 17.   xvii. 170.
de Corona
    34.   ii. 53 *n.*   iii. 45, 58, 59, 67, 76, 84, 94, 103.
    vii. 145.   xi. 94 *n.*   xiv. 85.   xv. 154.
Scorpiace x. 107.
de Idololatria vii. 45 *n.*   xiv. 93 *n.*, *bis.*
ad Scapulam ii. 27.   iii. 14 *n.*, 16, 128.
de fuga in persecutione xi. 46, 48.   xiv. 70, 169.

adversus Praxeam
    117, 118.   i. 117, 118.   ii. 97, 121.   viii. 122.
    xix. 122.   xxi. 123.   xxvi. 57 *n.*
de monogamia
    37.   x. 86.   xi. 181.   xvi. 53 *n.*
de jejunio
    37, 178.   ii. 94.   iii. 95 *n.*   x. 94.   xi. 169.
    xiii. 51, 95 *n.*   xvii. 46.
de pudicitia
    178.   i. 90.   ii. 91.   iv. 18.   vii. 79 *n.*
    ix. 60.   x. 52.   x. 79, 90.   xiii. 52, 61.   xviii. 90.
    xix. 61.   xx. 90.

www.ingramcontent.com/pod-product-compliance
Ingram Content Group UK Ltd.
Pitfield, Milton Keynes, MK11 3LW, UK
UKHW042143280225
455719UK00001B/56